THE HERRING FISHERS
OF WALES

The Herring Fishers of Wales

*A coastal journey of the Welsh shores
in search of King Herring.*

Mike Smylie

No. 6
WELSH HERITAGE SERIES

ISBN: 0-86381-467-0

First published in 1998 by Gwasg Carreg Gwalch,
Iard yr Orsaf, Llanrwst, Dyffryn Conwy, Wales.
☎ (01492) 642031

Printed and published in Wales.

All drawings by the author, except those by Lewis Morris, taken from
his 'Plans in St Georges Channel – 1748', and others as credited.

For the seas have I been accustomed
I will walk by sea and river
Along the strand with my circled net.

Maredudd ap Rhys (c1430-60)

My partner wrote this on a birthday card to me many years ago. From that time I decided that I'd write, and write about the herring fishery and more especially that of the country I live in, as it previously seems to have been forgotten. I, therefore, complete the circle with my very own net.

for Christoffer, my son . . . for all those hours spent waiting

This book is also dedicated to all the herring in the sea, and to the hope that man will begin to look after him, and others, that ring our shores.

Although much of the research for this book was of a primary nature, the author acknowledges the works of others that have proved invaluable. Primarily these are:

Wales and the Sea Fisheries by Colin Matheson – published by the National Museum of Wales and by the Press Board of the University of Wales 1929.

Aberystwyth Fishing Boats by R.J.H. Lloyd – published in the Mariner's Mirror Vol.41, no.2 – 1955.

Tenby Fishing Boats by R.J.H. Lloyd – published in the Mariner's Mirror Vol.44, no.2 – 1958.

The Welsh Port Books by E.A. Lewis (Cardiff – 1927) 1550-1603.

However, a whole host of excellently researched local history books can be found relevant to most parts of the Welsh coastline. These, too, have proved useful to a certain extent.

The author wishes to express his gratitude to those that have helped during the research for this book. These include the staff of both the Gwynedd Archives Office and the Anglesey County Record Office; Dr David Jenkins; Dick Evans; Hugh M. Lewis MBE; Gyto Jones; William Troughton and the staff at the National Library of Wales; David Jones, boatbuilder of Chester; Paul Raggett, Derek Huyton and Margaret Canby-Lewis, all of Solva; the staff at the Tenby Museum and the Nefyn Museum.

CONTENTS

Introduction – The King of the Sea

Herring – From the Teutonic word 'Heer' meaning Army.

The herring is but a small fish, which by no means reflects its huge impact upon mankind. It belongs to the 'clupidae' family of fish that includes the pilchard, sprat and anchovy, and together they form what has been described as the largest fishery throughout the world and make up approximately one quarter of all seawater fish landed.

Herring are pelagic, as are mackerel, tuna, salmon and sharks. This means they swim at or near the surface of the sea to feed on the plankton, very often out in the deep cold water of the ocean. However, at their spawning time, they swim in huge shoals into shallower water. Once at the spawning ground, the same ground where they were conceived, the female swims on her side depositing her eggs – on average 30,000 of them – on the sandy or stony bottom. She is followed by her male who fertilises these with his milt. Spawning occurs normally in the spring or autumn, although different species of herring spawn at different times, and others will spawn in summer or winter. Some species are even anadromous – they swim into freshwater rivers to spawn. The Cleddau herring is a perfect example of this (see chapter 1).

It is when the herring spawn in the shallow water or feed at the surface at night that they offer the fisherman his best chance of catching them. The shoals in which they swim are massive – sometimes 2 miles wide and up to twice that in length – so that even the natural predators – porpoises and herring whales – can merely nibble at the outer extremities rather than penetrate the dense mass of fish.

Herring are found in many parts of the world. The North Pacific herring is caught off the American West coast and off China and Japan. The North Atlantic species is found all along the American seaboard between Long Island and Labrador, and

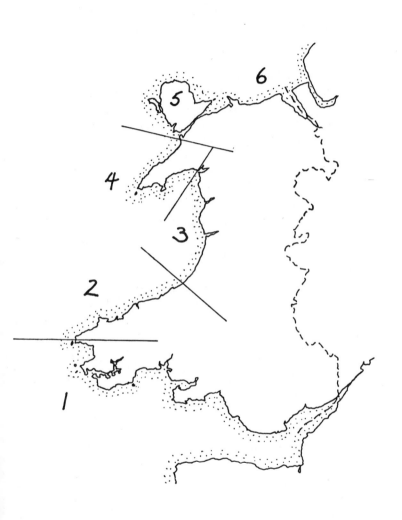

The Welsh Herring Fishers

up as far as the Greenland coast. On our side of the Atlantic they are netted in Iceland, Norway, the White Sea, Denmark, the Baltic Sea and the Bay of Biscay as well as all around the British Isles and Ireland.

In general the fish are caught by becoming enmeshed in drift-nets that are set at the surface of the sea by the fishermen from their boats. These nets can stretch for miles since the advent of motive power at the beginning of this century. Previously the sailing vessels with their hemp nets could only cope with a relatively small number of nets that are joined together to form a train of nets. After the introduction of cotton nets, which were a great deal lighter, a longer train was set. This increased again after steam winches were fitted to the craft, in the era just prior to the development of the internal combustion engine.

Trawling, however, has been adapted over the last one hundred and fifty years so that various methods are used to catch herring. Within Britain this has been mostly using a ring-net which is generally set by two boats to encircle the shoal and bag it into the net once the ends are joined. Other forms of trawling are employed in different parts of the world, and today's new super-trawlers are using new technology to make the catching of herring a financial certainty that ensures a return on the large amounts of money needed to build these boats. Within the Welsh herring fisheries, however, this is largely irrelevant.

Herring – an ancient food
The nutritional value of the herring has been long recognised. From archeological evidence it is clear that early man used it as a primary source of food. Centuries later the Romans found herring an important part of their diet. This seems to have remained the same until the twentieth century arrived with its depleted stocks and fast food.

The first actual fishery seems to have been off the East

Drawing by E. Prys Owen of fishing boats at Cricieth c.1830
photo: National Library of Wales

Anglian coast. The annals of the monastery of Barking, founded in 670AD, inform us that a tax was levied upon herrings known as the 'herring silver'. In the monastery of Evesham, founded in 709AD, there are references to the herring fishery upon the West coast. During the time of William the Conqueror, 60,000 herrings were paid to the king by the fishermen of Great Yarmouth, according to the Domesday Book. Evidence appears throughout the middle ages of a thriving fishery all around the East coast, and in Scotland there are indications of a busy export of herrings over 1000 years ago.

The first real 'great herring fishery' grew up around the shores of the South West of Sweden in the twelfth century. For over 300 years small boats – up to 7500 at one time – fished close inshore and landed at the various curing houses that were dotted all along the coast. The trade was controlled by merchants from, specifically, Lübeck and Bremen in Northern Germany, although other towns were involved. These merchants formed the Hanseatic League of Merchants and, in turn, became a hugely important political force wielding power in many countries of the globe. Their representatives were to be found in many dark corners, and in London they had a warehouse on the present site of Cannon Street Station, called the 'Steelyard'. They controlled every aspect of the fishery from the catching, to curing, packing and transportation. And the fishery was of such an importance that Rome itself decreed that work could be allowed on Sundays and other Holy Days. Such was the reliability of the currency of herring that merchants in Britain demanded payment in pounds of 'easterlings', which later became today's pounds 'sterling'. However, this powerhouse fell apart when the herring eventually defected by altering their migratory pattern, a change said to have occurred because of a huge increase in rainfall one year that coincided with unusually high tides. The herring, in the space of a year, deserted the Swedish shore and the Oresund, and flowed in their armies into the North Sea.

Holland, Scotland and England benefited mostly from this

change in habit. The Dutch fishermen for a period had complete control over the North Sea fishing with over 3000 of their 'busses – large sailing vessels with up to 15 crew that caught and cured the catch aboard – fishing at any one time, many within sight of the Scottish coast. However, with the introduction of bounties in the eighteenth century, the Scots fishery flourished, and the Napoleonic Wars saw the final demise of the Dutch command. Within a hundred years the Scots oversaw one of the most productive fisheries Britain has ever seen and one that reached its peak in 1913 when some half a million tons were landed in the whole of Britain.

It is against this background that the Welsh herring fishery, as we shall see, survived from the same early roots. Although it was dwarfed under the shadow of the North Sea, its socio-economic importance lies just as heavy upon the development of Wales over the last one thousand years. Three points, however, meant that the Welsh fishery did not evolve on the same scale. The growth of industrial mining and quarrying – most importantly in the field of coal and slate, although other products such as lead, copper and stone were extracted on large scales; the proximity of green fertile land to the coasts; and the lesser frequency of the shoals that appeared more erratic in their habits off the Welsh coast.

The Silver Darlings

Never has such another fishery attracted the attention of artists, writers and poets throughout Europe alike. Whether this attraction stems from their vision of fishermen as hunters who use their utmost skill in the detection of the shoals, usually at night, fighting uncertainty in the form of the weather and the whereabouts of the shoals, or the image of the beauty of millions of the glittering fish swimming in dark waters, on moonlit nights (although they swim closer to the surface at times of a new moon rather than a full moon), being caught and taken aboard small open boats, is unclear. But there is a wealth of writing that portrays the herring in its natural habitat, evoking its mystique and the ideas of hardship with comparisons to the American goldrush. Yet its history still lies veiled in the darkness of its secrecy and its truth unknown by the majority whose ancestors it fed. This book attempts to show that the reality of the once-proud herring lies all around us, if only we choose to spend a little time searching for it, so that we may possibly look briefly into the lives of thousands of our fellow men who helped create Wales into its present day shape.

TENBY CUTTER

CHAPTER 1

South Wales to St. David's Head

Tenby is fish! The town's Welsh name *Dinbych-y-pysgod* – literally 'little fort of the fishes' – reflects its position as the main fishing station along the South Wales coast from medieval times up to the latter part of the nineteenth century.

Its first quay was built in 1328 after Edward 3 gave the 'good men of Teneby' the rights to raise money for its construction by levying charges – quayage – upon its use. Before this time boats had had to draw up the tidal River Ritec into Pill Lake, at the back of the town, before beaching in the mud to unload. The town was an important trading centre as well as fishing harbour, due to its fine position and was well placed to trade with Devon and Cornwall, France and Ireland.

Fishing was just as important to the town's economy as was

the foreign trade. The fishermen paid tithes of herring and oysters for mass to be said on their behalf in the tiny St Julians chapel that sat on the harbour.

Huge amounts of herring were undoubtedly landed at Tenby throughout the medieval period. Pembrokeshire, it seems, was self-sufficient in its needs. However it appears that the fishery never developed its full potential, and, at certain times, was in decline.

The levels of fish imported and exported can be seen from the Welsh Port Books. In 1554 some Scotch herring was brought into Milford during a few years of scarsity. However, by the end of the sixteenth century, the majority of cured herring being traded was in export, by which time Tenby was sending barrels of herring to France, Ireland, Chester, Liverpool, Bristol and even Carmarthen (*Caerfyrddin*).

In his book *Description of Penbrokeshire*, George Owens, one of the county's sons and well-renowned native writers, wrote of the coast of the county as being 'enclosed with a hedge of herring' in the early seventeenth century and that 'these kinde of fishe is taken on the shores of this Countrey in great abondance'.

In 1553, the customs of Swansea charged a penny on every barrel of cured herring entering the port. Similarly Carmarthen imported cured herring from Clovelly and Barnstaple, the major centres for the Devon fishery, although at times, many Welsh boats did sail over to fish there. Clovelly was particularly renowned for its quality of herring. It also was imported from Wexford in Ireland. Tenby was the most easterly point along the South Wales coast that the herring generally swam, although a letter in the Peniarth Estate Books of 1798 notes that 'the merchants of Pembroke, Swansea, and all the coasts of South Wales from Milford Haven to the mouth of the Bristol river, about King Road, doing the same' – that is catching and curing herring and exporting it to the Mediterranean countries. Oysters were prevalent all along the coast, especially on the

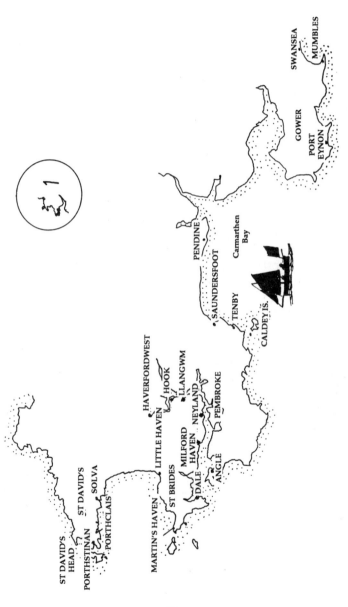

MUMBLES
SWANSEA
GOWER
PORT EYNON
PENDINE
Carmarthen Bay
SAUNDERSFOOT
TENBY
CALDEY IS.
HAVERFORDWEST
HOOK
LLANGWM
LITTLE HAVEN
NEYLAND
PEMBROKE
MILFORD HAVEN
MARTIN'S HAVEN
ST BRIDES
DALE
ANGLE
ST DAVID'S HEAD
PORTHSTINAN
ST DAVID'S
SOLVA
PORTHCLAIS

Gower peninsula where a thriving fishery emerged at Mumbles and Port Eynon. The various estuaries had their own cocklers, salmon fisheries and other inshore fishermen – for instance, Marrosse (near Pendine), which was a small village with a landing place in 1566, had two fishing boats called the 'Sondaye' and the 'Marye', both two tonnes apiece, and both were 'fysshing nere the shore'. It is probable that these inshore fishermen did, at various times, join in with the herring fishing, they being only a few miles from Tenby. Similarly, Saundersfoot was a sleepy little fishing village up to the end of the eighteenth century, after which coal seems to have occupied the harbour trade.

When Daniel Defoe visited Tenby in the early 1720's, he found it 'the most agreeable town on all the seacoast of South Wales, except for Pembroke, being a very good road for shipping and well frequented; here is a great fishing for herring in its season, a great colliery or rather export of coal, and they also drive a considerable trade to Ireland'. However, the fisheries in the town seemed by then to be in decline. In fact, 1750 seems to have been the time after which all the herring fishery of Pembrokeshire and Cardigan went into decline. Whether this was merely because of a greater consumption to satisfy the increasing population as Britain entered the Industrial Revolution seems uncertain, but perhaps it does best explain this so-called decline that never really seems to have resulted in a permanent closure of the herring fishery.

Interestingly, though, Tenby has its own tales about the herring's disappearance. One tells of a certain deaf and dumb beggar who was falsely accused of acting as a pirate's spy and was beaten very nearly to death by one local inhabitant with the unlikely name of Leekie Porridge. As he staggered away out of the town he cursed it, and the herring, from that moment, deserted these waters! Another story mentions a special rich fishing ground over a bank called Will's Mark. As the fishermen grew rich, they began to forget the marks enabling them to find

*Tenby harbour showing the Brixham and Dartmouth smacks
with Tenby luggers in the foreground
photo: Francis Frith c.1890*

*Tenby Harbour again showing the Devon fleet
with a few local luggers on the beach
photo: Tenby Museum & Art Gallery*

the bank, and after some years they lost the fishery altogether. An attempt was made to rediscover the bank, but to no avail.

Tenby had its quay rebuilt in 1842, yet by this time, the fishing in the town does seem to have been controlled by Devon fishermen. A more realistic reason for the decline in the fishing is that the poor fishermen were never able to buy themselves the bigger boats, so that they were unable to compete with the larger boats that came from Torbay. From pictorial evidence of the nineteenth century the harbour does seem to have been filled with these Devon trawlers, although the town did have its own fleet of small luggers.

These local craft are shown in drawings of the town from the early nineteenth century. They were about 20ft long, clinker built, probably locally, had two square-sails and resembled many other craft on the west coast that undoubtedly evolved through the Viking influence that played heavily on fishing boat design on the vast majority of the British coast. By the end of the nineteenth century they were bigger, with the largest built being the *Eileen* in 1891 at 27ft overall and 25ft on the keel. By this time the transition from square-sail to lugsail had occurred around the British coastline, the lug being merely an extension of the square sail, with the yard – the wooden spar along the top of the sail – being moved backwards at the point where it is supported off the mast. Thereafter these small vessels were called 'Tenby luggers', and there were up to fifty such craft working out of the harbour at various times. One feature of their design was contrary to their general Norse ancestry, this being the transom stern, the adoption of which was quite common along the Welsh coast, an influence most likely to have come from Devon and Cornwall, where it was supposedly imported from Brittany. A wider stern gave the boat more body, which in turn meant that there was more room to work and more space to carry fish. It was also safer when working over the stern tending lobster pots, a fishery of consequence in Cornish waters, and one of some significance along parts of this coast.

*The Tenby lugger 'Florence', M81, dressed overall on the beach,
presumably for an occassion such as the local regatta
photo: Tenby Museum & Art Gallery*

*A typical Tenby lugger under full sail
– this one is registered as M172
photo: Tenby Museum & Art Gallery*

Although initially clinker-built – that is the planks overlapped eachother – carvel construction was introduced by which the planks were laid edge-to on the oak frames, this again being a French influence. Larch, a native softwood, was generally used for the planking, this often being cut locally. An added advantage of carvel construction was that the boats could be built a greater length and were much stronger, and therefore lasted longer.

Their use continued into the present century, although it must be assumed that herring did not feature particularly amongst the fish the fishermen landed. Herring certainly went into decline before the First World War in 1914, although whether it simply deserted the British shores through migratory changes, or it was purely overfished, is still unclear. Probably it was a mixture of both as the new steam vessels were landing huge catches of the fish. The inshore fishermen, however, had to adapt, and all around the coasts tourism produced an ever increasing throng of holidaymakers who were only too keen to hire their vessels for a few hours. As we shall see all around the coast of Wales, the advent of tourism changed the whole face of the traditional way of life. The railway began this revolution in the mid-nineteenth century – although the rich came to Tenby prior to then to sample the medicinal benefits of the town's seawater, and the Tenby fishermen were more likely to be seen taking a group of trippers out to Caldey Island *(Ynys Byr)* rather than catching a boatload of fish during the summer season. Only during the off-season did they revert to their old pastime. This fact alone contributed to the continued use of the Tenby luggers, and so ensured their survival into this century. However, with changing attitudes and modern materials, wooden boats have ceased to be a viable option so that most were left to fall apart and now only one example of the type has survived. This lugger remains in the collection at the Welsh Industrial and Maritime Museum at Cardiff awaiting restoration.

So far in our intended journey around the Welsh coast we

Brixham trawlers anchored off Tenby c.1890
photo: Tenby Museum & Art Gallery

St Julians Chapel on the Pier Head by Charles Norris

have remained in Tenby, that capital of the herring fishery along the south coast. Short incursions can be made towards the east, although historically, as we've seen, the herring was of no significance. One slight exception might be Port Eynon, on the Gower peninsula, where there are the remains of a salthouse built to extract salt from the sea. The bay supposedly abounded with similar salthouses and herrings are supposed to have been landed and cured here, although the village is more renowned for its oysters, crabs and lobsters than it is for herring. Also, as already mentioned, herrings were landed at Swansea and mention is made in the 1878 'Report of the Sea Fisheries of England and Wales' of herrings being taken in the bay at Swansea in September, although pollution from the smelting works is said to have ensured this didn't often occur. Landings were also made by steam trawler into Cardiff after about 1870, yet these landings are of very little consequence as they were just as likely fished off the Devon coast, or out towards the Irish coast. In the eighteenth century, herrings were supposedly taken off what is now Porthcawl, although at the time the area was inhabited by only a handful of folk at Nottage and Newton. The docks at Porthcawl, and the subsequent building of the town, did not happen until the following century to ship out coal from the nearby pits. Newport, in 1884, was reported as having no fishing boats.

Moving westwards it is a short distance to the wonderfully sheltered waters of Milford Haven. Here the Cleddau waterway bites deep into the Pembroke coastline. A distinctive herring fishery emerged in the upper reaches of the estuary, centred on the villages of Llangwm and Hook. The herring itself was a sub-species, and it entered the estuary waters to spawn in winter, it being unique amongst the British herring to swim so far up such a waterway to do this. It was fished using 16ft open rowing boats, known as compass-net boats – the compass-net being primarily used to take salmon and sewin (seatrout) – that were always tarred inside and out. At Llangwm, this was centred around the inlet suitably named 'Black Tar', and it

Tenby lugger by Doug Perry after Charles Norris

*A typical Llangwm fishing boat
as used in the local herring industry
photo: unknown*

survived into this century. The Llangwm fisherwomen were renowned all around the local towns to where they walked several times a week with the catch of the day, whether it be herring, oysters, shrimps, cockles or salmon. These women controlled the selling of the entire catch, there being no merchants here. They were recognised by their colourful tweed dresses, aprons and black felt hats, and spoke their own dialect of Welsh. One of the women, Dolly Palmer, became famous for her strength and beauty, and she was even interviewed by the Daily Mirror!

Even as far upstream as Haverfordwest *(Hwlffordd)* – whose name derives from Haver Fjord after the Vikings settled there in the eighth century – there were boats that caught herring, open like the Llangwm boats. George Owens says of the town 'the greatest and plentifullest markett of the shire . . . And for fishes it passeth all others in Wales, without anie comparison, both for plenti and varitie'. Together with Pembroke and Tenby, these were the three chief herring stations of South Wales in the fourteenth century.

Further downstream, Neyland had been a herring station since the mid part of the nineteenth century, after the railway arrived in 1853, and probably much before this time. However, the whole picture of the herring fishery, indeed much of the fishery of South Wales, changed with the opening of the Milford Haven dock in 1888. Although the town had only been founded a century before, and some of its earliest settlers were whalers from Nantucket, keen to develop the market for whale oil to light the London streets, it obviously quickly grew, with Brixham boats landing there throughout the nineteenth century. The first fishing boat to land there after the new docks were built was the *Sybil*, a steam trawler of 98ft in length. The story of the development of Milford Haven is one in itself, and there are good books that concern themselves solely with its growth: here it is suffice to say that the harbour was built to attract the transatlantic liners that plied their track to and from America. The entrance of the *Sybil* as the first ship was not exactly as

A group of Llangwm fisherwomen. They were once seen all over Pembrokeshire with their baskets full of herrings and cockles photo: Museum of Welsh Life, St Fagans

Buck print of Haverfordwest Priory & quay – 1740

planned, but it became obvious within a short period of the opening of the dock that it wasn't to be the transatlantic ships that were to frequent the harbour but fishing boats. Steam trawlers and drifters were increasingly commanding the trade, forcing the smaller sailing vessels out of business. Within a few years of the opening, some 55 steam trawlers and 200 sailing smacks were based in Milford Haven. At about the turn of the century it gained its first four herring drifters with the arrival of *Girl Daisy, Boy Fred, Cato* and *Favo*, owned locally, and within another year there were 40 such vessels. By 1904 this had amazingly increased to 200 drifters. The first smokehouse was built in 1908, with four more coming after the impending war. By 1925 the port was the principal herring station in England and Wales, with 124,000 barrels of herring being landed during the previous year, 4000 of which were even sent to the East coast of England, where the mother of all English herring fisheries occurred each autumn. In terms of the amount of fish being landed, Milford peaked around 1946 when some 59,000 tons were landed, and thereafter the port slid slowly into decline. However it did enjoy a brief respite when, in 1963, some 45,656 hundredweight of herring was landed, this temporary increase in landings being generally attributed to the Scottish drifters that found the port convenient. Today the once proud fishdock has been turned into a marina, another unfortunate result of the slow disgression into an 'English way of life'.

Before we leave this area the other small fishing communities with a history of herring fishing must be mentioned. When the Bishop of St David's *(Tyddewi)* wrote, in 1595, of Milford Haven that 'the sea-coasts nere about it yeld plenty of fish' he wasn't just referring to the waterway itself. All around the tiny coves and hamlets between St Ann's Head and St David's Head there were based one or two, or more, small craft. This is further substantiated by George Owens again, referring to the herring – 'the places of their takeing in this shire most usuallie was in Fishguard *(Abergwaun)*, Newport

Milford Haven Docks c.1890
photo: Tenby Museum & Art Gallery

The beach at Martin's Haven c.1930, showing both transon-
sterned Tenby luggers and double-ended boats, all clinker built
photo: author's collection

(Trefdraeth) and Dinas (which we will see in the next chapter), where for manie years, and even from the beginninge there hath some quantite beene yearly taken, of later years they have resorted to Broade havon, Galtop roade, Martin havon, Hopgain, and St Brides, and have beene plentifullie taken to the great Commoditie of the Countrye, and nowe in the yeare 1602 they have been taken within Milford havon, and in the Roades of Tenby and Caldey, and neere St David's, and generllie in everye parte of the sea shoare about this shire from the fall of Tyvy to Earewere'. This fishery saw an upsurge in the nineteenth century, especially after the Government introduced bounties upon fish landed by small boats. When bounties were initially introduced in 1750 (bounties were in fact introduced on exported herring in 1705), they were only paid on the tonnage of the boats that went herring fishing. There were certain requirements – the boats had to be sufficiently large, decked and had to group at one of a few ports around Britain – so the consequence was that the small boats were discouraged from fishing. To set the balance right, in 1787, a bounty was introduced for herring taken by open or half-decked boats. The inshore fleets developed rapidly after this, with 2/8d being paid per barrel of white herring landed, 1/9d for a barrel of full red herring and 1s for empty 'spent' herring. This payment survived until 1830.

Talking of the bishops of St David's, about 1550, the current bishop was one Robert Ferrar who was later burned at the stake for heresy. However, commenting on the scarcity of the herring, he blamed the greed of the fishermen who, he said, took too many fish at times of plenty, thereby ensuring that they didn't breed. This sort of opinion sounds familiar today!

Such places that were home to small fleets were Dale and Angle within the Milford Haven. Those places as mentioned by George Owens can still be identified in the most. Martin's Haven is the stepping off point for Skomer Island, and is also the traditional harbour of the Marloes fishermen where once

30

Solva harbour with the 'Norseman' on the left
that belonged to the Aberaeron Steam Packet Co
photo: Margaret Canby-Lewis

The harbour at Porthclais
with one clinker-built fishing boat drawn up
photo: Paul Raggett

there were 20 fishing boats operating; St Brides Haven is a picturesque hamlet with a tiny chapel, where in 1707, there was an 'Olde Cellar or Fishouse' and where nearby there was a house built 'for the purpose of making fish and cellaring and keeping of goods'. In his book 'Portrait of Pembrokeshire' Dillwyn Miles states "St. Brides was renowned for its herring fishery. A little chapel, built by the sea, was used, when it became ruinous, to store salt for the curing of fish – thus:

When St Brides Chapel a salthouse was made,
St Brides lost the herring trade."

Goultrop Roads are to the west of Little Haven, home to a tiny fleet, with Broad Haven just to the north. Around the other side of St Brides Bay, noted for its herring fishery in the nineteenth century, the small hamlet of Solva lies nestling amongst the rocks. When writing of his travels of about 1540 in *Itinerary in Wales*, John Leland noted 'Solvach – or Solverach – a small creke for ballingars and fischar botes'. Its creek is probably better known for its smuggling antics than its fishing, but there seems little doubt that herring were landed here at various times in its history. Salt was a most popular smuggling commodity, and, according to local historian Paul Ragget, one of the local magistrates was sympathetic to their cause and often warned the smugglers prior to his inspecting their craft, so that it was reported that "the salinity of the water in Solva harbour was significantly increased after one of his visits"!

Continuing along the coast, the little refuge of Porthclais was built as the harbour for the religious community of St David's and its cathedral, and here, too, a small fleet of herring boats were based during the autumnal herring season. One mention here was in the St David's Port Books of 1566-1603: "11th April 1566, the 'Le Marie De Porto Milford, whose agent was Alex Watkins of St Davids', landed 1 last emptye cask". This must have been 12 empty herring barrels which, when full, make up about one last. However, like most of the other trading coves, limestone burning and coal importing was more important to the local economy, the fishing providing a welcome alternative to crop tending, especially during the quiet part of the agricultural year. Porthclais's harbour wall is reputedly Roman, and in 1566 the harbour had a couple of boats of some 8 tons with 4 crew that 'tradeth to Ireland, North Wales and upp Severne afishinge'. Indeed, reading through the list of *Ports and Creeks of Wales in the Sixteenth Century*, it appears that many of the 'barkes' from places such as Carewe, Llanstinan, the Steinton parish, Dale, Pembroke and Neverne went up the River Severn 'afishinge'. At the same time 'Goultrop and Bridebay' had an estimated 6 households, 'Solvaich' and 'Porclays' none while 'Tenbie' had an estimated 200. Llanstinian, or Porth Stinian as it is now known as, has for generations been the landing place of pilgrims going to St David's. More recently it is the departure point for Ramsey Island, and is home to the St David's lifeboat. It is also the home of several potting boats that work this coast for crabs and lobsters. It is, therefore, possible that herring was once landed there.

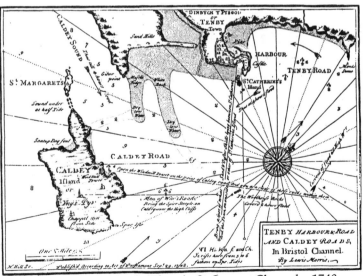

map from Lewis Morris 'Plans in St Georges Channel – 1748

CHAPTER 2

St David's Head to Aberaeron

Passing around the headland of St David's, the first landing with a history of fishing is at Abereiddi where, like Porth Stinian, crabs and lobsters are the sought-after fruit of the sea. However it is not beyond imagination that herrings were landed here too in older times. Afterall, it was said at one time that no creek or bay was without its herring fleet. Although there is a safe anchorage for small boats at Abereiddi, this was only formed after a narrow passage was blasted in the wall of rock into the foot of a large slate quarry that had earlier been worked. Previously any boat landing would have had to work directly off the beach.

Continuing northeast now, another relic of the Welsh

N

ABERAERON
CEI-BACH
NEWQUAY
CWMTYDU
LLANGRANNOG
PENBRYN
TRE SAITH
ABERPORTH
CARDIGAN
ST DOGMAEL'S
NEWPORT
CWM-YR-EGLWYS
FISHGUARD
GOODWICK
ABERCASTLE
PORTHGAIN
ABEREIDDI
ST DAVID'S HEAD

quarrying age can be seen at Porth-gain. Originally the tiny cove was home to an equally tiny fishing fleet: the present Sloop Inn dates from 1743. However, as the slate quarrying seems to only date back to 1837, this can perhaps suggest that the hamlet was home to a few herring fishermen and smugglers. Bricks were later made from the crushed slate, and then stone quarried to produce chippings and stone setts for the road building program that was gearing up around the country, with the substantial harbour dating from about 1850. At one time it was producing some 40,000 tons of stone a year. However, like much of Wales's industrial past, it lies dormant, a relic of a once proud age that is wholly forgotten and ignored. Porth-gain could, with imagination, be re-created into something atmospheric, a place of beauty standing as a memorial of the link between this past and today's rush yet still retaining a degree of its charm. But it won't, as to do this would necessitate profit, and that in itself would mean attracting masses of income in the form of tourists, which would in turn destroy that which was being rediscovered. Perhaps, then, it is best for it to be quietly left alone, so that those few who do make the effort can reflect on the peace that now blankets this harmonious little spot.

Abercastle is a pretty little cove, again with its slate quarry, limestone kiln and tiny harbour where ships were once built. It was home to a few herring boats in the eighteenth century, and probably earlier.

The herring fishery of Cardigan Bay was clearly flourishing during the reign of Elizabeth 1, Lewis Morris, in his *Plans of Harbours, Bars, Bays & Roads in St George's Channel* of 1748 says of the herring in the bay that 'this is one of the greatest Fisheries in Wales'. At Goodwick *(Wdig)* there was a tiny pier where boats were landed while just around the corner, at Lower Fishguard, another small fleet landed, so that the two rivalled eachother. Salted herrings, wool, skins and slates were exported from the harbour at 'Fiscard', where Lewis Morris observed 'Between this place and Newport they cure yearly about a

Porthgain harbour 1997
photo: author

Abercastle
photo: author

thousand barrels of herring'. Fishguard was, in fact, only second to Haverfordwest in the export of herrings up to the early eighteenth century, when red and white herrings were exported to the Mediterranean countries, according to Fentons "Pembrokeshire". It declined in the following century.

Goodwick's fortunes altered when the railway from the south arrived in the 1890's, albeit 50 years after Brunel had first planned to make Fishguard a port for the Irish ferry. When the Irish potato famine struck in 1846, the business-like Victorians cancelled the project. This suited the navy who were worried about invasion after the unsuccessful French landing of 1797 – Britain's last invasion – at nearby Careg Wasted. Although Brunel did continue his railway building briefly, changing direction to Abermaw, home to a couple of fishing boats, by 1853 he had again altered course, and had taken his 'iron road' to Haverfordwest. When at last it did arrive here all those years later, the pier at Goodwick was demolished to make way for the new terminus. Briefly the town enjoyed the benefits of transatlantic liners calling, but the dreams of becoming a transatlantic port withered away after the First World War. Fishguard's Lower harbour, on the other hand, continued as a fish port, although by this time most of the herring had disappeared.

Pwllgwaelod is a tiny beach near to Dinas Head where herrings could have been landed, and probably were at sometime. Across the isthmus of the Dinas promontory is the tiny landing place of Cwm-yr-eglwys where herring was landed up to the nineteenth century. A lease of Dinas Island, dated 1825, now in the National Library of Wales in Aberystwyth, demands, as well as £170 a year and '6 fat hens at Shrovetide', all the customs of herring landed by the fishermen. The same lease also mentions that 'poles for the drying of nets' may be erected on the foreshore 'as is usual and custom'. Newport, as we've already seen, was an important herring station. Here the Welsh Port Books show there were 20 households in 1566, the same as there were in 'Fiscard'.

The harbour at Lower Fishguard
photo: Francis Frith collection

The Old quay at Goodwick
photo: Tenby Museum & Art Gallery

Cardigan *(Aberteifi)* consisted of 55 households in 1566, according to the Port Books. These also give us a good description of the vessels common around the bays: ' . . . we have no shippe belonging to eny of the sayed havons crikes and landinge places (Cardiganshire) or eny other bottes or vessels other than smale shippinge bottes conteyinge 4 or 5 tonnes apice wich use to fyshe apon the cost of the sayed shire and do use non other trad and that chifly heringe physshinge after Michelmas; in everi of the sayed botted duringe the fysshinge tyme are continually 6 or seven persons all fysshermen and no mariners'. In other words they were no ships along the coast other than those required for 'fishing near the shore'.

However Cardigan developed between 1678 and 1709 into an important herring station. Barrels were imported from Wexford, and after being filled with salted herring, they were then sent back to Dublin. In 1701 Cardigan exported 1072 barrels, and in 1782, 1734 barrels. Many of these were sent by boat to the Pickle Herring Quay at Southwark, in London – the herring centre of the capital to where herring had been imported since the days of the Baltic herring in the fifteenth century. Afterall, it is said that many Welshmen went out to join in with this fishery that developed on the Southwest Swedish coast, where the German merchants took absolute control. Cardigan also sent cured herring to Bristol, Exeter, Falmouth, Dartmouth, Chester and Liverpool. One cargo even went as far as the Canary Islands.

During the eighteenth century the herring fishery encouraged merchants and mariners into the area, timber was imported for boatbuilding, and sailmaking, ropemaking and anchor smithying were firmly established as thriving businesses. The port peaked at its zenith in the mid-nineteenth century when it had 78 boats employing 400 men. However silting up was by then becoming a problem, and already the herring fishery was being centred more at St Dogmael's *(Llandudoch)*, just across the river. For a time the herring boats were kept at the 'Netpool' at Cardigan, while across the river

Cwm-yr-Eglwys showing the remains of the chapel
that was washed away by a violent storm in 1859
photo: author

Typical Cardigan fishing boats
photo: unknown

they were beached at the 'Pinog'. St Dogmaels, however, soon surpassed Cardigan and became one of the principal herring ports for Wales, not far behind Aberporth, which, as we shall see, was the major port in Cardigan Bay.

Aberporth lies a few miles up the coast from Cardigan, and was described jointly as 'Item theris too Crikes at Aberporth and Pebr[in] in the sayed coyntey [Cardiganshire]' in 1566. Why it grew into the principal herring station in South Wales is not clear. Lewis Morris identified it as Cribach Bay in 1748, stating that a pier would help the herring fishery, so that the fishing was obviously flourishing then. However no pier was ever built, and the boats continued to land directly onto the beach. Like the adjacent villages Tresaith, Penbryn and Llangrannog, the ships were left laid up at Cardigan while the mariners spent their time catching the herring. The fish was cured on the beaches, and much of it was exported to Ireland. However Sgadan Aberporth – literally Aberporth herring – became popular amongst the growing towns of South Wales where it was thought to have a particularly subtle taste. Herring, by this time, was an established part of the national diet, it being extremely nourishing and tasty. Llangrannog established itself as a religious settlement upon the strength of its herring fishery.

It is probably fair to say that herring from the four hamlets together was classed together under the collective name of Aberporth herring, thereby explaining how a tiny beach landing could become the premier herring port of the Bay. Group the produce from four such communities and this is quite plausible.

Today each of the old hamlets are quiet, that is as far as fishing is concerned. But the two sandy beaches at Aberporth – Traeth y Plas and Traeth Dyffryn – bustle with visitors in summer and the village is regarded as a resort with its associated caravan parks, self-catering chalets and guest houses. The first visitors came towards the end of the nineteenth century and the first regatta was held in 1909 to create swimming and boat races and other traditional seaside games, finishing with a firework display, all to encourage a notion of

Captain Evans alongside a Cardigan-registered herring boat
photo: Welsh Industrial & Maritime Museum, Cardiff

The beach at Aberporth with a herring boat sailing off.
Note the smaller boat sailing off close to the rocks on the other side
photo: National Library of Wales

43

relaxation and fun. Llangrannog has suffered the same fate although perhaps not on the same scale as Aberporth, and thankfully, the two beaches at Penbryn and Tresaith remain, on the whole, unspoilt. However, the ghosts of the herring fishermen must no doubt pace these beaches at night wondering at the spectacle of sandcastles and brightlights where once only herring barrels stood.

The Aberporth Herring Boats

In Cardigan and St Dogmaels the boats were reported about 1830 as being 8 to 20 tons burthen with masts and sails, mostly open and manned by 6 or 8 crew. Similar boats were used all along this coast, and especially at Aberporth, from where they took their name. These herring boats were between 25 and 30f overall, and were beached because of the lack of harbours along the coast. Indeed the whole coast lacks proper harbours, as was noted in 1884: 'from Milford Haven to Holyhead there is not a port into which a boat drawing eight feet six inches of water can run at all states of the tide'. Building of harbours was suggested so that the Welsh fisheries could compete with that of Scotland or East Anglia, but by then, I fear, the herring fishery had collapsed sufficiently so that this wasn't a viable option.

The boats were generally transom-sterned for reasons already discussed. Carvel construction also gained precedent in the nineteenth century, so that the boats were heavily built. They were mostly used for drift-netting for the herring – locally called 'drifio', and they drifted with the incoming tide from the Cardigan estuary back home with up to 25 nets, each 50 feet long, attached as a long wall of netting for the herring to swim into and become enmeshed. Drift-netting was mostly carried out at night or in the early morning, when the herring came close inshore and up to the surface to feed, they preferring to do this in the dark. However the fishermen did work a fixed net known as 'tranio' or 'setin', which involved setting a net about three fathoms deep at the surface using floats to keep it there, and small stones to weight the bottom so that it hung in the

Another view of Aberporth beach,
this time with three herring boats pulled up the beach.
Note the sails drying on one of these boats
photo: Welsh Industrial & Maritime Museum, Cardiff

Nets drying on the quay at New Quay
about the turn of the century
photo: author's collection

water. The ends were anchored in place and the advantage c
this method was that the net could be shot in dayligh
Sometimes only one end of the net would be secured so that
could turn with the current. Each fisherman would have hi
own favourite spots, but generally they wouldn't set the net to
far from home.

These herring boats mostly had two masts with lug sail
and the sails were only used to get to the fishing grounds. The
were never used while drifting for obvious reasons. At som
time in the nineteenth century, possibly when carv
construction was adopted, the rig was altered. They then set
gaff mainsail with a sprit-rigged mizzen. The sprit-rig wa
commonplace amongst many other coastal fishing communitie
prior to the nineteenth century, it being easy to work, and man
boats from the northern part of Cardigan Bay (Bae Ceredigion
used it. Some of these later boats even set a topsail to increas
their speed back from the herring grounds to land. Once th
railway had arrived in Cardigan the herring could be sent to th
railhead by horse and cart, so that the boats that landed firs
normally sold their catches for the best prices.

Boats of a similar design worked out of Fishguard an
Newport. In the north, the Aberporth type of boat was to b
found at Newquay (Cei Newydd) and even Aberaeron. By th
turn of the century numbers of these craft were declining, s
that by 1905 there were none left. Unfortunately now not on
example of these small, hardy little craft exists, which
considering their strength, is surprising.

Returning to our journey northwards, the coast hereabouts i
extremely remote, which made it perfect for smuggling. Larg
amounts of salt were brought in to the country illegally becaus
of the differentiation between the price of salt in Ireland an
that of it in Wales. Cwmtydu is a tiny cove along the rock
coastline towards Newquay, yet it seems to have thrived o
both the herring and smuggling, with French brandy bein
another of its main 'free-trade' goods.

Newquay itself was a smuggling centre too, it bein

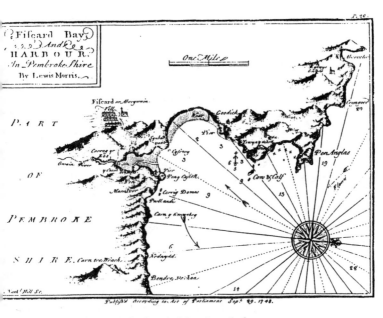

map by Lewis Morris as before

described in 1795 as a place of 'infamous notoriety' as it gave shelter to these smuggling vessels that brought in brandy and tobacco to be disposed of at Lampeter and Tregaron. However in 1566 there was a creek at 'Lanina' – which is actually Llanina Point, just around from Cei-bach – Little Quay – a couple of miles further up the coast. Here at Cei-bach the fishermen first landed at the tiny natural harbour that lies in the lee of Llanina Point with herring being included from early times. Ships, too, were built here near the two wooden breakwaters that were erected, the earliest documented ship being the 36 ton sloop 'Betsy' that was built in 1805, and the largest being the 'Syren' at 291 tons, built in 1887.

At one time the 'new quay' was going to be built at Ceibach, but the site to the west was favoured and so Newquay grew. Lewis Morris mentions it as a hamlet with small fishing sloops. The herring was 'of very superior quality'. The main pier that exists today was built after the harbour act of 1835, and was used extensively by the part-time fishermen. For like those from the south, the fishermen here worked the land throughout the rest of the year. Some were mariners that came home for the autumnal season, the story being the same all along Cardigan Bay coast so that there were no full-time fishermen until the advent of the twentieth century, with its powerful motorboats, easy access to markets and thriving trade in lobsters, crabs and scallops, many of which are now exported to Europe.

Aberaeron dates back to 1145 as a settlement, although its harbour wasn't built until 1811. It was identified as being 'a small Crike or landinge place' in 1566, and appeared to have been a thriving fishing community, no doubt fairing well on the herring which was a major export by 1750 – along with grain and lead-ore from the rich mines near Lampeter. After the harbour was built, there was based a fleet of herring boats that numbered over thirty vessels in the 1830's. Indeed the harbour became a major herring port, with the fleet increasing to over sixty boats towards the mid century, 'while several hundreds of strange boats came for the fishing', according to one report. Although much of the town's growth can be acknowledged to the growth of this herring fishery, the harbour also had its own flourishing shipbuilding, as well as the normal coastal import and export. The town itself was built in Regency style, with uniform Georgian houses facing geometrically laid out roads of standard width, with squares and terraces, and street names such as Wellington Street, Waterloo Street, Queen Street . . . all reflecting Britain's growth in the world, not that of Wales. Although tourism does feature in the town today, with the harbour having more yachts than fishing boats, it has retained some of its charm that most certainly did grow on the back of the meek herring.

CHAPTER 3

Aberaeron to Tremadog Bay

Although George Owens in his *Description of Penbrokeshire* was vastly impressed by the extent of the herring fishery around the coasts of that county, he would probably have been even more impressed had he viewed the fishery further north.

Between Aberaeron and Aberystwyth there are several communities that are relevant to the herring fishery. First of these is Aberarth, one of the oldest settlements along this entire coast, where boats were built until the builder moved to Aberaeron in 1847. Llansantffraid Llanon is a 'landinge place' according to Lewis Morris and where 55 ships were built at the Peris Yard before its closure in 1865. Two miles further north lies the village of Llanrhystud, also described as a landing place. However these three villages do have two things in common – they lie on a very fertile plain on the coast and consequently had, and still do have, a thriving farming trade, and, secondly, each village still has the remains of fish traps – 'goredi' – on the foreshore. Herring is assumed to have been

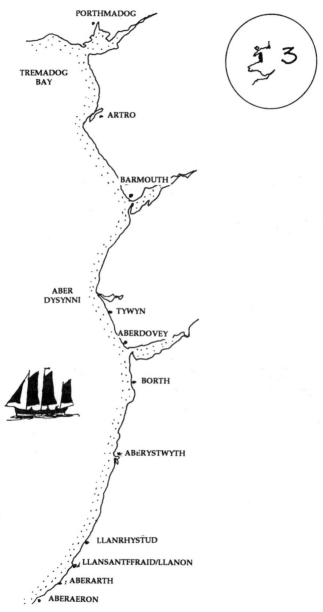

PORTHMADOG

TREMADOG
BAY

ARTRO

BARMOUTH

ABER
DYSYNNI

TYWYN

ABERDOVEY

BORTH

ABERYSTWYTH

LLANRHYSTUD

LLANSANTFFRAID/LLANON

ABERARTH

ABERAERON

landed here, both from boats that we have already seen worked out of every creek along Cardigan Bay, and from these fish traps. These semi-circular, stone-walled structures are covered by the sea at high tide, but then drain as the tide ebbs, trapping the fish which are unable to swim out against the tide. Once there were 12 traps at Aberarth, two of which were used up to the 1930's, while both Llansantffraid Llanon and Llanrhystud only have one or two examples.

Arriving now at Aberystwyth, where the rivers Ystwyth and Rheidol tumble down to meet the sea together, it is perhaps difficult to visualise that here was the very centre of the Welsh herring fishery in the middle ages. For in 1206 it was written in *Brut y Tywysogyon* (The Chronicle of the Princes) 'that year Maelgwn ap Rhys built the castle of Abereinion. And then God gave an abundance of fish in the estuary of the Ystwyth, so much that there was not its like before that'. Huge amounts of this herring, for that is what it presumably was, were landed in Aberystwyth which was merely a creek then. Records inform us that, in 1302, fishermen were being fined for selling herring below the highwater mark to escape paying market tolls. Others were fined for fishing without the requiste licences for their boats. The rights of the Crown had to be acknowledged by the fishermen whose normal arrangement was to pay five score herrings each time they went out. This later became an annual payment of £1 10s, and this payment became known as the 'Pryse, or Castle, Maes of herring', hence becoming the 'prisemes'. Later, when the Nanteos family held the lease, the first herrings caught in the bay each year were sent to the Nanteos estate (three miles to the southwest of the town). Later that century there were twenty boats working out of the creek. In 1566 Lewis Morris found a 'havon or landinge place at Aberystwyth being a bard havon . . . wherein shippes and vessels reparinge to the sayd port were acostomed to lad and unlad . . . ' The town remained an important herring station in the seventeenth and eighteenth centuries, with herring tithes of

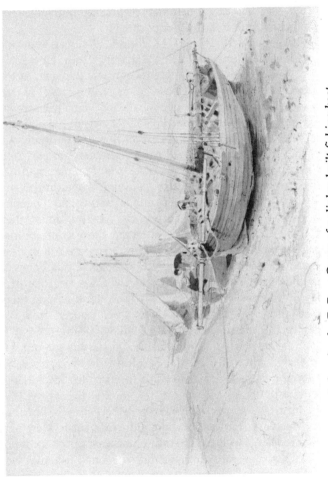

A drawing by E. Prys Owen of a clinker-built fishing boat at Aberystwyth in 1830
photo: National Library of Wales

about £1 being paid for each boat in the harbour. The list of tithes paid in September 1730 clearly states that there are 24 boats that paid the herring tithe. These all had English names such as 'Success', 'Maria', 'Hopewell', 'Providence' and 'Dove' – much like those found in any other port.

However Lewis Morris, in 1748, found 59 sloops working out of the harbour and another 38 jointly from Newquay, Aberaeron, Aberdyfi and Borth. He recognised the state of the poor harbour and reckoned that 'at least one half of the Seatown is lost for want of a good harbour'. Furthermore he noted that the bar is often choked up so that vessels have to stay in the harbour until the two rivers are in flood to let them out. He notes that the herring fishing begins in September and lasts three or four months. Other than herring, the chief commodities of the place are other species of fish, lead ore, wool, timber and oak bark. Of the 59 sloops that were either used to catch herring or to transport the herring during the season, most then reverted to normal coasting work carrying these commodities or importing coal. With regard to fishing boats, he found that, in one night on the 5th October 1745, 47 boats – this being as many as could get out of the harbour that tide because of a heavy sea on the bar – of about 12 ton each, took among them 2160 meises of herring, which at 126 to the Hundred, and five Hundreds to the meise, amounted to an incredible 1,360,800 fish, which, he calculated, would take 1,111 barrels to cure. He reckoned that catches of this size, which would be comparable to those caught in the North Sea, were sustainable if they had a convenient harbour.

Lewis Morris also recognised that Aberystwyth herrings supplied 'the very middle of England with fresh Herrings, which they carry off in great Quantities, at least equal to, if not more than what they cure'. Shrewsbury was one place that was documented as receiving herring from here. Other than herring, he notes that very few pilchards were landed, observing philosophically that this only shows that fish, as well as men, have their own particular Countries allotted them. Pilchard

Beach boats ashore at Aberystwyth
before the building of the esplanade – c. 1880
photo: National Library of Wales

Boats on the beach about ten years later. The transom stern of these
craft resemble many other craft of South Wales and even across to
Clovelly in Devon where the 'picarooners' had the same
pronounced wine glass transom
photo: National Library of Wales

fishing was the domaine of the Cornish fishermen until the early twentieth century, and obviously this was so in the preceding centuries. During the herring fishery, he noted that they also had a glut of cod, whiting pollack, whiting, rays and other fish which they put little value on.

The harbour was improved slightly between about 1836 and 1850, although the question of access at all tides was never really confronted. Evidence of this lack of development into the harbour facilities is apparent from the 1878 'Report of the Sea Fisheries of England and Wales'. Its writers – Frank Buckland and Spencer Walpole – came to Aberystwyth and interviewed several fishermen amongst others. Two of these expressed a willingness to pay harbour dues for the sake of better facilities, as at that time they were paying nothing. Thomas Cooper reckoned it wasn't a harbour at all, although he did call it a harbour of refuge not one of safety, and noted that he paid 10s at Whitehaven (Cumbria), and that he would be willing to do the same here.

The same report gives a good insight into the fishing of the middle part of the nineteenth century. One smack-owner Humphrey Owen, recognised the great herring fishery of 30 to 40 years ago, but said that the old people thought there was a curse now because the herrings had been used as manure at times of glut. John Jones mentioned 53 mease being caught by one boat with a fleet of 16 'old hemp nets' in 1831. He reckoned that the shoals deserted the coast about 1840, and accounted for this because of the increase in mining thereabouts that in turn caused pollution in the river thus preventing the herring from spawning, as they used to do, just outside the harbour, usually in October. However, this was denied by John Jones Attwood the solicitor for the Corporation, who said that the pollution did not drive the herrings away. He lived at Aberaeron, and reckoned that the herrings had deserted the whole coast. He remembered 60 mease of herring being brought in there, selling at 5 shillings a mease. He also reckoned that the shoals were beginning to return. John Gibson, editor of 'The Cambrian

*The three-masted tripper boat 'Lizzie' with a full compliment of
passengers just about to leave the beach there
photo: National Library of Wales*

*The nobby 'Snowdrop' alongside the quay at Aberystwyth
with fishermen sharing out the catch of herrings ashore
photo: National Library of Wales*

News', recalled watching the water 'boiling' with little fish like sprats and herring. He had watched them for five hours and mentioned large quantities that were being landed at Pwllheli.

The pictorial evidence of a fishing boat in Aberystwyth is from a drawing by E. Prys Owen from about 1830, now in the National Library of Wales. It depicts a clinker-built boat of about 25ft in length overall with bluff bows and a transom stern. Being slightly larger than those from further south, it had a small foredeck and a transverse beam to divide the hull into two different working areas. This boat was cutter-rigged with a mainsail, a jib and staysail set on a long bowsprit. The main boom extended well aft over the transom, while the mast was stepped against the foredeck which was well forward Although it has on its starboard side a beam trawl that shows it must have been trawling in the bay, it most likely drifted for herring in the season. This boat resembled many other that were common around the Irish Sea, and the shape of the hull reflects the influence of the Viking period.

By the time the railway arrived in Aberystwyth in 1843, the influence of the merchants from Liverpool and Hoylake was imposing itself upon the design of the larger boats in use in the port. These Lancashire nobbies, carvel built with their steeply raking sternposts, little sheer and cutter rigged, of between 25 and 40 feet, were common all around the coast of the Northwest of England, indeed the North coast of Wales. They worked off the town in the season, whilst at other times they might work off the Isle of Man. According to the fishing registers there were 83 boats registered in Aberystwyth in 1872, 2 of these being first class boats of over 15 tons, while 6 were second class, the remaining being third class – that is those under 18ft other than those navigated by oars alone. Probably most of the second class boats were of the nobby type. By 1883, when the town was described as 'the most considerable fishing station in Cardigan Bay', there were 9 second class boats totalling 60 tons.

In contrast, there were some 52 small herring drifters working from the town between this time and the end of the nineteenth century. These were between 20 and 25ft in keel length, with 3 being over 30ft. The earliest documented evidence of this smaller type of vessel is shown in a drawing of 1844, yet it is assumed that they were in use before this time. It has been suggested that they did in fact originate from the village of Borth, an ancient fishing community above the beach, a few miles north of Aberystwyth, where Lewis Morris found a small landing place in 1566. These craft had three masts, making them unique amongst the Welsh fleets, with the two forward masts having boomless gaff sails while the mizzen had a spritsail. They were clinker-built, undecked with transom sterns. These boats, built locally, usually from yellow pine and larch below the waterline, were ballasted with shingle from the beach which was discarded as the boat filled up with fish. They were also very lightly built, which resulted in them not having a long working life. Around the end of the 1880's, double-ended versions were introduced by a local builder, David Williams, who worked in Queens Road initially until he moved to his yard at Trefechan, on the south banks of the River Rheidol within the harbour. Although primarily built to take trippers out when the town seethed with visitors in the summer, the fishermen, who largely controlled this business, soon adapted them for fishing during the herring season.

Before long, the size of these double-enders was reduced to about 18ft overall. David William's sons continued his business and they reverted to the clinker method of building to enable them to produce lighter craft. These were primarily rowing boats, although they sometimes set a single lugsail, especially when going out in search of the herring. They were popular amongst the fishermen who often sailed them long distances, carrying a crew of two with 6 or 8 nets and there were 'a considerable number of them' at the turn of this century. The yard of David Williams and Sons eventually closed in 1959.

Another type of herring boat found all along this coast was the gig. Gigs were common in many parts of Britain, especially Cornwall, where they are still raced today amongst the coastal communities. The herring gigs of Wales were similar to the three-masted boats, between 16 and 21ft in the length of the keel, and were clinker built. The smaller gigs set a sprit mizzen when they rode to their drift-nets, while the bigger ones set two sprit sails, with a few having a gaff mainsail. Like the other craft, they too were used to ferry trippers around the bay.

Many of the Aberystwyth fishermen believed that the herring shoals moved from south to north, as they did at Aberporth as well. However, they had to sail to wherever the shoals were, and sometimes that meant only a short trip of a couple of miles, while at other times they had to sail as far as Newquay in the south or up into the Northern bight of the Bay by Porthmadog and Cricieth. They would sail in groups of up to 20 boats to set their nets at sunset. Leaving them in the water for an hour, they would then haul the first net to see if they had caught anything. If the catch was looking good, all the nets would be hauled in and they would sail home, as, with no working space aboard, they were unable to empty them. Otherwise they would be left for another hour. Sometimes the catch was landed directly onto the beach, and other times they used the harbour if the tide was high. The fishermen sometimes hawked the fish around the town, and, in later years, the whole catch was bought by the Liverpool merchants and put on the train and sent direct to the market there.

One story tells of an open boat in Tremadog Bay that took aboard an immense haul of herring so that it was so heavily laden that its 'oars floated out of the rowlocks'. It had to leave some of its nets behind and it just managed to make Pwllheli without sinking!

The herring fishery of Aberystwyth staggered on into the twentieth century, the decline being apparent in all corners of the Bay. However, in 1928, there were still three rowing boats in the local fleet, yet it is presumed that these did not survive 'at the herring' for more than a few years.

After the lack of enterprise in the town which resulted in the

*Barrelling the herring on the Aberystwyth quayside
photo: National Library of Wales*

*The herring fleet drying the sails of the nobbies in 1910 at Aberdyfi
photo: Hugh M. Lewis MBE*

harbour not being improved to encourage the growth of the fishery there, it's surprising to discover that private enterprise has today managed to invest some £8 million in re-developing the harbour. This has been described as superb high-class development with a marina and the proverbial shopping and residential units, and the harbour has been dredged to allow all the plastic yachts and such twenty-four hour access. This alone means that, for the first time ever, there will be a place of shelter between Milford and Holyhead accessible at all states of the tide. How ironic, then, that it has taken the empty face of capitalism and the promotion of tourism to provide such investment that could, if undertaken two hundred years ago, have resulted in the town becoming Wales's foremost fishing port into this century, and which, in turn, would have led to a complete transformation of the face of this town.

Carrying on north, past the aforementioned beach at Borth, the river Dyfi acts as a boundary between the north and south of the country. Crossing it at the first point at Machynlleth – although the railway crosses it further downstream – and travelling along the north side of the river, at one point almost at the water's edge, the first fishing station back towards the sea is at Aberdyfi.

The Port Books of Wales of 1565 describe 'Devye' as 'being a Haven and havinge no habitacion, but only three houses whereunto there is no resorte; save only in the tyme of hearinge fishinge at which tyme of fishing there is a wonderfull greate resorte of ffyshers assembled from all places within this Realme with Shippes Boottes and Vessels, and during which abidinge there, there is of the said cumpanye there assembles one chosen among themsellfes to be their Admirall. And there is nother Shippe nor Vessel that belongeth to the same Haven otherwise aforesaid, whereof we have deputed David ap Thomas ap Rutherche, and Thomas ap Humffrey beinge the substanciallest and nerest to the same haven'. In 1748 Lewis Morris notes that 'here, and at Borth, they have some years a good herring fishery . . . ' In 1834 Aberdyfi was a small, quiet fishing village with nets often drying on the foreshore, smacks on the beach and a plentiful supply of herring, salmon and mackerel, as well as mussels, crabs and lobsters. During the West Wales famine of 1649, Aberdyfi herring was sent to South Merionethshire and West Montgomeryshire. The wharf and jetty were built in 1882 to enable slates to be loaded from the nearby quarries. Fishing smacks from Devon and Fleetwood are said to have unloaded fish there, probably after the railway arrived in 1867. Several transom-sterned skiffs worked off the beach, and these were built locally. Shipbuilding also flourished on the beach. A photograph of 1910 shows four or five gaff-rigged nobby-type boats with their sails drying sitting on the beach. These boats fished for both herring and mackerel in deep water.

Aber Dysynni is a small inlet north of Aberdyfi where there was a creek 'with no habition or resort' in 1565. Likewise Barmouth *(Abermaw)*, was a haven with no habition, but only 4 houses, according to the same report into *The Havens and Creeks of Merioneth*. It also mentions that there were 'But only towe litle Bootes that the said Res ap Res and Harry ap Eden' [owners of two of the houses] do use to cary men over that Passaige . . . ' In other words it was merely a ferry landing across the estuary. However this is strange as it was reported that Barmouth was in fact one of three of the main herring stations of N. Wales in the mid-fourteenth century and, to back this up, Lewis Morris found a healthy herring fishery at the port two hundred years later. Salted herrings had remained an important element of the local diet, though it is noted that the herring fishery was much depleted at the port by the 1840's – the 'Hungry Forties' – so much so that they had to be imported into the area after this time.

The Peniarth Estate lies a few miles north along the road from Tywyn, which has a meagre mention of herring being landed. An entry in the Estate books, already mentioned, is thus: 'In July 1770, I reached the Post-house in Dolgellau on Sunday . . . the first Herrings that came to the town was the second week in September and all shotten; the slender supply continued in that state till October, about the middle of the month: then they became many full-roed, and delicious when taken at Nefyn in Caernarfonshire so late as the end of November, and have not altered these twenty six years, till the present, it being the 19 day of September and not a single fish arrived . . . On the 6th October the first herring were brought to market 1796, and sold at a penny each, but shotten, and again on 7th, 10th, 12th, 15th, 18th, 21st, 22nd, 23rd at the reduced price of a half penny from the 21st to the 29th of October inclusive. But in the month of Dec 16, I bought three as fine full-roed fish for two-pence taken at Barmouth, as ever were eaten, and again on the 23rd the same number at the same price but one only soft-roed – In the memory of the oldest inhabitants there never were taken any at this time at Barmouth in such perfection; I consider it a blessing and as such insert it'.

Both Aberdyfi and Barmouth were thriving ports, exporting huge amounts of oak bark into mainly Ireland, although some of it was also sent to Scotland. The majority of this was used in the leather tanning process, but some of it might have been used within the herring fishery thus:

The nets the fishermen used were made from cotton which rotted easily in the saltwater. Consequently it was necessary to treat the nets occasionally to preserve them. To do this efficiently, they were barked in a liquid preservative which was made up from a solution of water, oak bark and various other ingredients. These included milk, rancid butter or fish oils, all of which helped the preservative to hold onto the cotton. Cotton sails were treated similarly both to treat the material and to colour it. Sometimes even horse dung was added to the mixture to help fix the colouring. Dyes were used in some parts of the country, and different regions had different recipes. During the mid-nineteenth century the oak bark was swapped for imported cutch which originated from India, coming from the bark of the acacia tree, and which was deemed more effective in preserving

Landing the catch at Barmouth in about 1880
photo: author's collection

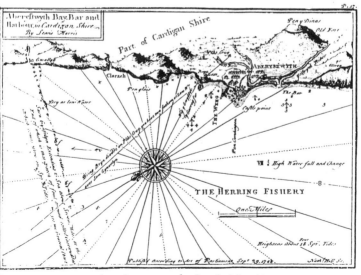

drawing – map by Lewis Morris

the cotton. Once man-made materials were used for the making of nets and sails this process became obselete.

Looking through the records of ships that traded with both these ports, it is worth noting the price of herring and comparing it with the price of other goods at the time:

	Year	Qty	Item	Cost
	1701	½	Hundred of herring cost	1 4d
	1785	4	Hundred of herring cost	15s
March	1804	1	Hundred of herring cost	5 6
March	1804	1	barrel of herring cost	£1 15 9
March	1804	1	lb of sugar cost	9d
March	1804	12	lb of beef cost	6s
July	1806	1	cwt of herring cost	6s
Sept	1806	1	cwt of herring cost	5s
Oct	1806	1	cwt of herring cost	9s
Oct	1806	1	cwt of potatoes cost	3 9d
Oct	1806	1	gallon of whisky for ship's store cost	8s
Feb	1807	1	cwt of herring cost	7s
May	1807	1	cwt of herring cost	8s
May	1807		pilotage out of Aberdyfi cost	7 6d
Feb	1809	1	cwt of herring cost	8s

Sweeney Hall lies on the outskirts of Oswestry, some 5 miles east of Barmouth. Its Estate Papers of 1677 include a serie of letters from Edward Lloyd, who refers to 'his herrings', an reading through these letters made me believe he was som form of merchant. One letter to Mr N. Thomas was dated 1 October 1677: ' . . . there is such a quantity of herring (y) coas tho not yet come down to you, but upon their voyage I doub not but you receave (y) and be prepared to salt a considerabl quantity, if you can not get salt, if you boile (y) in sea-water i my great kettle till halfe be consumed it will serve rarely for (y first pickle'. Where he was fishing is unclear, but it is to b assumed that it was either at Barmouth or Aberdyfi. M Thomas probably was at Aberystwyth or the Cardigan area. I' love to know how big the 'great kettle' was!

North of Barmouth, Morris identifies a small creek at Artro, although there are no dwellings there, no resort nor any ships, boats or vessels. This creek is the inlet at Llanbedr, and is sandy and tidal. Morris also notes a creek at Ytraeth Mawre, which, as Artro, had nothing. This was the estuary at what is now Porthmadog, and the waters were shoal and dangerous, and so were to be avoided. The herring never came this far into Tremadog Bay, and so the fishermen had no need to be there. Porthmadog developed at Wales's premier slate port in the nineteenth century, when ships came to load slate and take it to the four corners of the world. Fishing, then, was an unnecessary occupation, even in the herring season, as work either in the quarries, in the harbour or on the countless vessels was in constant demand.

— ABERDARON FISHING BOAT — Anesuyué —

CHAPTER 4

The Llŷn Peninsula

The Llŷn peninsula sticks out like an arm with a hand grasping at the harvest of the sea. It remains pretty much as inaccessible today as it has done since man ever came to these shores, mainly because the mountainous bulk of beautiful Snowdonia confronts the traveller in his direct route here, so that he must go around this barrier, either to the north or the south, to reach the rich, wonderful land of Llŷn.

Throughout the ages man has found it easier to arrive and depart by sea. Although the Llŷn man has his fertile land to live by, it is always to the sea he gazes when his thoughts wander to

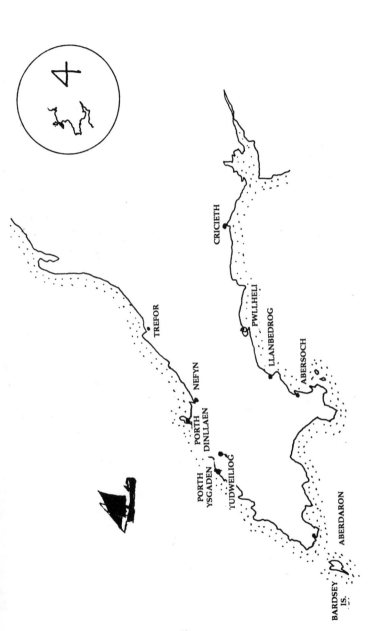

CRICIETH

PWLLHELI

LLANBEDROG

ABERSOCH

TREFOR

NEFYN

PORTH DINLLAEN

PORTH YSGADEN

TUDWEILIOG

ABERDARON

BARDSEY IS.

the outside. Ships have traded here for generations, and hamlets have grown up all along the seaboard. And, of course, it has been to the sea he has gone to gather the fish to supplement his diet.

Cricieth is the first place we arrive at as we head around the coast of this green land. Here, under the ancient castle fortified by Edward 1, several clinker-built herring boats would have been found up to the First World War. These are depicted in a drawing by E. Prys Owen of 1831, being some 20-25ft long, having two masts and either sprit-rigged or gaff-rigged it seems, and a transom stern. One is shown with three masts. Cricieth herring were well known, but unfortunately they were generally regarded as inferior to the Nefyn herring, those from the north side of Llŷn being of a superior tasting. To add insult to injury, it was said that Cricieth herrings 'are cured in the village, but, I fear, with no great attention or skill than what are but too commonly bestowed upon them in the county' according to Edmund Hyde Hall in his *Description of Caernarvonshire* 1809-1811. He also noted that 'some trade in the export way is however carried on by the sale of herrings taken in the adjoining bays by half-decked vessels of scanty tonnage and limited number'.

Of Pwllheli, the Welsh Port Books tell of a port or haven having a town with 36 cottages with an obviously thriving coastal trade, although he finds no ships there belonging to the town. One of the earliest mention of herring is as part payment of one mease of herring for the lease on a piece of land in the thirteenth century. By the beginning of the eighteenth century, there was a good deal of salt being discharged into the growing port, and to confirm this, cargoes of herring were sent to Liverpool, Dublin, Milford Haven and Carlisle. In 1748, Lewis Morris found a healthy herring fishery, and its strength is supported by the inventory of a certain blacksmith's will of 1774 that showed he owned 'two boats, a large net, four herring nets and a large rake to Harvest oysters'. This shows that most fishermen were part-time, as elsewhere along the coast, and

Herring boats on the beach at Criccieth c. 1890
photo: National Library of Wales

nobby alongside at Pwllheli discharging
photo: Gwynedd Archives

that a thriving oyster trade was alive in the town. Herrings, as elsewhere, would only be sought in season.

Heavy catches of herring were reported around the mid-part of the nineteenth century, and herrings sold for 2/6 per Hundred in 1844. On December 2nd 1848, the Caernarfon and Denbighshire Herald reported thus: 'Pwllheli – on Wednesday last, upwards of 8000 fine herrings were netted and brought in here by the crew of the Fishing Boat *Wylan*, Owen Lewis, master'. Large catches of mackerel were also reported as being caught, receiving extremely high prices. In 1857 there were plentiful supplies of herring at the Pwllheli market, and by this time many fishermen from the Wirral were frequenting the place. This is backed up by the evidence from the editor of 'The Cambrian News', as mentioned before. During 1880, there were about 400 fishermen from the Isle of Man in residence in the town, participating in the autumn herring. Fishermen from Cheshire were reported there again in 1896, and, presumably, they must have always borne influence on the fishing. This is again apparent in that the nobby gained precedent against the more traditional type of small herring boat as was found at Cricieth, most likely due to the fact that the harbour facilities were much better, and could be accessed at most states of the tide, although not at low water.

There were low years though. In 1878 the fishing completely failed so that a relief fund had to be set up for the penniless fishermen. In early 1879, £64 was raised through a house-to-house collection, and this was given out in the form of £40 worth of food to the 50 or so fishermen who were in need, the balance being held over in reserve in case of further failure. However this was obviously unnecessary in the short term as the Caernarfon and Denbigh Herald confirms on 23rd October 1880: 'During the past few days there have been large takes of herrings at Pwllheli, which were at once packed in barrels and sent away. On Friday several waggon loads were thus consigned'. The herring indeed was a haphazard fishery!

By 1889, there is no doubt that the herring fishery in the port

*The beach at Aberdaron with fisherman raising the sails
on his small beach boat
photo: Gwynedd Archives*

*Herring boats on the beach at Bardsey Island
photo: National Library of Wales*

was in sharp decline, there being only 15 fishing boats belonging to the town, although this had again increased to 20 by 1892. It seems that the Cheshire fishermen still visited, as was reported in 1896, and probably accounted for much of the fish landed. Statistics in the fishing returns to the Western Sea Fisheries Committee show that Pwllheli was the most important port within its jurisdiction in that its tallies of fish landed, excluding shellfish, in the years 1890 and 1891 far exceeded those of Holyhead *(Caergybi)*, Caernarfon, Bangor and Aberystwyth & Aberaeron.

The nobbys remained fishing from the harbour until the 1920's, with lobster fishing gaining over the herring, and after that decade there seems to have been a distinct cessation of all fishing. Again, as in Aberystwyth, a new marina today sits in the main channel that was once a bustle of vessels sailing in and out of the harbour, but which, today, is filled with boats that have absolutely no beauty when compared to the pretty little skiffs and stumpy nobbys of one hundred years ago.

Continuing westwards, the small beach at Llanbedrog is reputed to have had a couple of herring boats working off the beach. Some three miles further west lies Abersoch, a small inlet within the St Tudwal's Roads, protected by a headland. Here in 1566 the Welsh Port Books describe: 'Stydwalles, a wyld rode and landinge place where divers shippes do repair without habitacon upon the same and in the Qwenes maiesties governance'. With its sheltered little harbour, the herring fishery offered a pleasant alternative to the farming year, and so several nobbys would be found dried out up the river during the latter months of the year. However, as Pwllheli provided better landing facilities, not much herring, other than that for local consumption, entered the so-called harbour.

Aberdaron sits at the far end of the Llŷn peninsula, Wales's very own Land's End, and one which is by far more inaccessible than the Cornish one. Indeed it must be one of the most remotest places in all of England and Wales. Nestling between two headlands, the tiny village has associations with the sea, its only neighbour, for as long as anyone can remember. That these people have been fishing for centuries is undisputable. The rich herring grounds stretch both north and south, and from here in the sixteenth century herrings were landed and some exported to Ireland and Chester, although the majority of those landed seem to have gone for local consumption. In the next two centuries they were reported as being taken to Liverpool and London in the small vessels that were loaded on the exposed beach.

By the end of the eighteenth century the herring export flourished alongside other goods such as slate, butter, bacon, cheese and kelp. Many boats, too, brought in salt, although, as elsewhere, this was often as an unofficial import. As herrings formed such an important part of the people's diet, salt was in ever demand. Because of the salt duties imposed by government, salt was 4d a pound in 1750. The same salt cost 1d per lb just across the water in Ireland, so smuggled in salt costing 2d a lb was an obvious choice. This was often brought in, stashed as ballast, by the many slate-carrying vessels that visited the area. When the salt duties were abolished in 1825, the need for smuggled-in salt disappeared. However, the practise of free-trade continued, and still does today, and probably always will while there still is a desire for tobacco, brandy, drugs . . .

The boats used by the Aberdaron fishermen were, at one time, double-ended craft with which they fished with drift-nets. These can be seen to have a Viking influence reaching directly back to their incursions into the area in the eighth and ninth centuries. These sort of boats survived well into the nineteenth century until the herring declined. Lobstering gained preference, there being rich stocks of the shellfish off the rocky coasts of Llŷn, especially along the north coast, so that the design of boat altered. The fishermen adopted the transom stern to enable them to work over the stern when hauling their pots. Previously, many a boat had capsised when hauling a pot in over the side or at the pointed stern. The boats also had a deep skeg aft so that they could be rowed backwards onto a pot. Because the fishermen had their own tiny creek of Porth Meudwy that afforded some shelter, they didn't have to always launch into a surf, an impossible task with a transom-sterned vessel.

Many of these boats were built locally by John Thomas, on Bardsey Island, where a small community of farmers and fishers lived. He had been building ships on the beach at Aberdaron, and fishing in the boats of David Williams of Aberystwyth, until he began building them from his own design. His son continued the practise into this century, and many of his boats still race at Aberdaron in the summer, the oldest in the fleet being the 'Annie', which was built incredibly in 1865. Originally lug-rigged, they adopted gaff-rig around the turn of this century, and now, mostly, support gunter rigs.

Journeying back up the north coast of the peninsula, the inquitious traveller can find several havens where herrings were once landed, albeit in small quantities. The first, Porth Iago, is a tiny inlet, where even today a couple of potters work from. At Tudweiliog, the fishermen used four creeks, Hall noting 'the shore of the ground is notched into several small creeks, as Porth Tywyn, Colmon, Gwylan and Ysgadan, in all of which ply the vessels engaged in the herring fishery, in pursuit of which they are said to frequently stretch over as far as the Irish coast'. Salt, he noted, for the curing of the fish was allowed duty free 'here as elsewhere'. Although the salt duties hadn't been abolished, it seems that for a while salt was exempted to encourage the curing of herring. Most of the herring taken here were for local consumption. The writer Thomas Pennant reports that in 1771 herrings were taken in abundance 'from Porth Ysgaden, or the Port of Herrings, to Bardseye island. The value of this catch was normally some £4000. The catch was either salted ashore or taken direct to Dublin by Irish wherries'. Porth Ysgaden still remains a remote sandy beach with a couple of crab boats working from there. Porth Colmon, according to Hall, was only used occasionally for 'shelter to the boats when

A huge load of herring at Nefyn
photo: Gwynedd Archives

A typical double-ended herring boat from Nefyn
with a catch being landed c. 1900
photo: Gwynedd Archives

pressed by the storm during the season of the herring fishery'.

The boats that worked these creeks were 25ft long, and were similar to those from further up the coast as we shall see later. However, the practise of landing at such remote spots just goes to show that the fishermen would use every cove, every beach possible to land herring, as, in season, the shoals were huge and there was plenty of fish for all.

Nefyn lies about half way down the Llŷn peninsula, and is lucky to have two sheltered beaches. Both Porth Nefyn and Porth Dinllaen, a mile west of the former, provided excellent refuge from the exposure of the Irish Sea and both were bases to free fisheries, according to the lease of Cefn Amlwch in 1742. Porth Dinllaen has an arm that sweeps around to provide shelter in all but the northeast wind, and so was the favoured of the two landings. Up to the nineteenth century, the majority of the herring was in fact landed there, with Hall reporting that curing stations lined the bay.

Herring was obviously landed here in the middle ages: in 1287 it possessed 63 fishing nets. In 1565 it was noted as a landing thus: 'Portynllayn, a creke havyng a town nere unto hit called Nevyn having in the same 17 households'. In 1680 local inventories of the people state:

Einion ap Addach – 9 oxen, 6 cows, 20 sheep, 3 heifers, 3 fishing nets.

Ieuan ap Madoc – 4 oxen, cow, horse, heifer, boat and 4 nets.

Llywarth Crun – 1 cow, 1 net.

Bleddyn Fychan – 6 oxen, 3 cows, 2 horses, 1 small boat, 3 nets.

Tagwynstl wraig Addaf – 2 cows, horse, heifer (9 years old), 1 net.

Dai Bach – 2 sheep, heifer, 2 nets.

The fishermen thus farmed throughout the main part of the year, turning to the herring during the season between September and January. Occasionally, if the moon was right, they might begin fishing in August, although some believed that it was wrong to begin prior to Thanksgiving day

Richard Jones mending his nets at Nefyn c. 1935
photo: Gwynedd Archives

Robin Lloyd and others landing herring from their nets at Nefyn
photo: Gwynedd Archives

Fishermen everywhere were superstitious, and in Wales they were particularly religious.

When Lewis Morris visited the place prior to him publishing his book in 1748, he found a thriving trade and a useful pier for the herring fishery that had been built by Contribution, chiefly by the generosity of William Bodvill MP. The previous year, 1747, he found that nearly 5000 barrels of salt herring were disposed of, besides that needed for the local consumption.

Nefyn herring became renowned throughout Wales, and the port became the principal herring port of the north. In 1679, Nefyn supplied the nearby Glynllifon estate with herrings, which, according to the Estate Books, cost between a shilling and 14d a Hundred. The cry of 'Penwaig Nefyn' became common throughout the northern half of the Principality, and indeed far beyond. Furthermore, the herrings here were reputedly twice the size of those Cricieth variants.

The herring boats here were about 18ft long, double-ended to enable them to work off the beach and came from the builder 'Matthews' of Menai Bridge. Hall noted some 40 boats, each owned by seven men, all of whom were either agriculturists, traders or seamen. About the turn of the century they cost about £20. The fishermen used fixed nets here, either anchoring one end or both, depending at what point off the shore they were fishing because of the tidal currents. At Y Gamlas they anchored both ends, while at Y Swangins only one end was fixed. Another factor to affect the herrings' movement was the moon – a new moon often meant that the herrings came close inshore. It was unusual for the fishermen to sail far for the herring, although it has been said that occasionally they went as far as the Irish coast.

The Nefyn fishermen used a net that was about 50 yards long with a one inch mesh net, and one enterprising chap acted as a net merchant in the village. For fishermen who could not afford their own nets, he would loan them, taking a quarter of their catches in payment of this service.

Scotch-built herring fifies at Porth Dinllaen c. 1885
photo: author's collection

Sign above the 'Three Herrings' house in Nefyn 1995
photo: author

The fishermen of Gwynedd had an unwritten rule that ensured there were no disagreements concerning fishing limits – that no fisherman from one village would ever fish within another's ground.

The herring fishery continued in Nefyn into this century, and in 1910 there were some 40 boats working from the port. However this seems to have been completely wiped out after the outbreak of war in 1914, both because of the war and the decline in herring, so that fishing from the port never recovered. Although the place has retained its charm, even with tourists patronising its beauty, today there are no reminders of the fact that this was once 'the' herring station of North Wales.

Moving on again northwards, the only landing place of any significance before we leave Llŷn is at Trefor. Here a quay was built when the Eifl Quarry opened in 1850. Tracks were laid down from the stone quarry, and wagons were pulled to the quay by a small locomotive – 'loco bach'. However, herring fishing was exercised from the port, but only on a very small scale, probably by the workers from the quarry when the shoals were in. In 1900, there were 20 fishing boats based there, and this had fallen to 8 by 1950. Even today, some of the folk who worked at the mine remember herring being landed for consumption by those at the quarry-workers' settlement of Nant Gwrtheyrn. Furthermore, a lifeboat was based at Trefor between 1883 and 1901. More recently, the quay has been restored and now remains as one of those very unspoilt parts of the coastline of rural Wales.

Before we leave this part of the coast, perhaps a mention of the ways that the fishermen found the shoals of herring is appropriate. Before the days of fish-finders and other navigational and electronic aids, the fishermen only had their natural senses to find the fish. Although they had an excellent local knowledge of the ground beneath the water, this wasn't always enough. Herring, as their nature leads them, are an erratic fish, who often shift their swimming patterns because of tidal changes, weather conditions and, as mentioned, the phases of the moon. Being pelagic, they come to the surface at night to feed, and more so at the times of a new moon, or cloudy weather. Hence the fishermen learned to watch for the sign of the herring – the natural appearances. They watched for the natural predators of the fish – the porpoises or diving gannets – and for other signs such as oily patches in the water or phosphorescence below the surface. Basking sharks, which feed on the same plankton as herring, were another sure sign that the herring were in the vicinity. All in all, he had to draw on a vast wealth of knowledge only gained through experience to seek his prey that was as canny as him in avoiding detection, if not more so.

In the Buckland and Walpole Parliamentary Report of 1878, they calculated that, in total, fifty times the amount of herring that mankind catches in Northern Europe is taken by its natural predators. Assuming 2.4 billion fish were caught by net, then 120 billion are eaten in the seas. Assuming one fish survives for each killed, and half are female, that leaves some 60 billion females to spawn their 20,000 eggs (a conservative estimate), which calculates to 1,200,000,000,000,000 eggs produced. Therefore, to keep up with those that are lost, only one in every 10,000 eggs needs to hatch into an adult fish.

One reminder of the past is the oath of a packer of fish from the Nefyn Corporation Book of 1815, and consequently I have copied it below:

The Oath of a Packer of Fish

'You shall well and truly swear to execute the office of a Packer of Fish within the Porth of Porthdinllaen, in which you shall see that White and Red herrings shall be packed in lawful Barrels and Vessels and shall be truly and justly laid and packed and shall be of ONE saying or drying and equally well packed in every part of the Barrel or Vessel, and you shall also see that all Codfish and other salted fish shall be packed in the said Port, shall be truly and justly laid and Packed and you shall also see that everything belonging to the said Office of a Packer be well and truly executed within the Port aforesaid, according to the best of your skill and knowledge.

So help you God.'

CHAPTER 5

The Isle of Anglesey

Driving onto the Isle of Anglesey *(Ynys Môn)*, over either Telford's famous suspension bridge, or that fixed bridge of Robert Stephenson, the small island of Ynys Gorad Goch can easily be seen at its lonely stance in the Swellies – that particular stretch of water between these two bridges that is locally renowned for its treacherous tides and sharp rocks. On Ynys Gorad Goch there remains one of the best examples of a fish trap or weir, although it probably never resulted in much herring being taken in it. These weirs were common all along the Menai Straits, as on other parts of the Welsh coast, as we've already seen. Others can still be seen around Menai Bridge. However, travel east along a beautiful stretch of wooded road to Beaumaris, where King Edward's castle sits serenely overlooking the Straits with the backdrop of Snowdonia, and here you will find the medieval centre of Anglesey's herring fishery. Before Beaumaris and its castle were even thought about, in the thirteenth century, what was then the small hamlet of Llanfaes was home to a thriving trade in the fish, and was in fact the chief herring port of the North Wales coast. Most of the herring here were caught in weirs, although some was caught by boat. The herring migrates close to the shore at Beaumaris, and is said to spawn over the sandy seabed in late winter or early spring.

In 1294 at Llanfaes, a custom of 1 penny on every mease of herring landed was charged. Furthermore, every herring boat entering or leaving the port owed the king one mease, worth about 2 shillings. This fact confirms that there were several vessels that were catching herring further out to sea, probably outside of the Menai Straits, although this is pure conjecture. The money raised no doubt went towards paying for the castle, which was completed the following year. As a form of thank you, the entire population of Llanfaes was, in 1303, forcibly moved enmasse to Rhosyr, which then became called Newborough, some ten miles away.

Fishing in Anglesey, as it was amongst most of the other coastal regions of the Principality, was a part-time occupation of the farmers. Although Anglesey, The Mother of Wales, is in general terms fertile, the herring fishing presented those that worked the land as an alternative at a time when the land was quiet. Given the proximity of the shoals to the shore, and its abundance at times, its taking was a relatively easy pursuit. However, as again in other parts of the coast, its migratory patterns might easily mean that it would desert a particular popular area for no apparent reason.

Anglesey's herring fishing never seemed to develop its full potential. In the sixteenth century Leland wrote that 'there is a good commoditie for fishinge about Tir Mon but theire lacketh courage and diligence'. Whether this was, infact, the truth behind this lack of potential is unknown. It is equally as likely

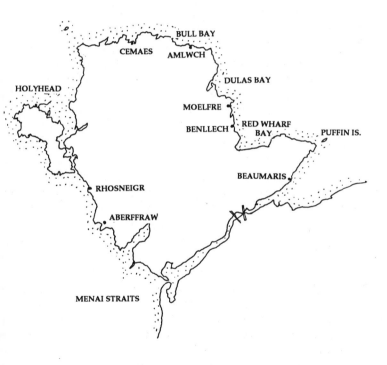

BULL BAY

CEMAES   AMLWCH

DULAS BAY

HOLYHEAD

MOELFRE

BENLLECH   RED WHARF
                BAY   PUFFIN IS.

BEAUMARIS

RHOSNEIGR

ABERFFRAW

MENAI STRAITS

that the farmers of the fertile land had no reason to prosecute the herring to the fullest extent. The fish caught merely served as a variation in their diet and its supply around the surrounding areas was not necessary to those that caught it. However, one traveller suggested another reason, he describing Anglesey as 'naked and unpleasant' and as not producing 10% of the possible yield that it could. However, after living on Anglesey for very many years, I certainly would not describe it as 'naked and unpleasant' – to the contrary in fact.

The Welsh Port Books of 1550-1603 show the extent of the export of herring from the island, and the amount suggests that a further development of the fishery occurred in the sixteenth century. Salt was brought in from the Cheshire saltmines via ship from Chester, with salted herring being sent back to the port, or sometimes on to Liverpool. Herring certainly must have been an important part of the local economy in Beaumaris in later years as in 1722 and 1723 the town elected two men – Lewis Davies and Richard Morris – as the official fish packers there.

In 1798, Warner wrote that huge shoals 'sometimes visit the Anglesea coast, which are taken, dried, and exported; being considered by the knowing ones in delicacies, as particularly excellent'.

The herring has continued to swim up as far as Beaumaris. In the 1920's one local inhabitant who was reportedly a great herring fisherman of unsurpassed knowledge was said to have been able to tell exactly when the herring were in. He'd 'just look in (the air), give a sniff, and he'd tell you when they'd be there' said his nephew Harold Jones who later became coxswain of the lifeboat there. His other uncle was reputedly a successful prawn fishermen who sold these by the pint from his home to visitors.

As recently as 1997 herring have reportedly been taken by line and feathers from Gallows Point in the spring and off both the east and west coasts of the island during the summer. Gallows Point is the promontory west of the town where local condemned prisoners were hanged, and where, in the nineteenth century, many ships were built.

Travelling further along the gentle shores of the Menai Straits, one comes in time to the tip at Penmon, with Puffin Island some distance across the channel. Puffin Island has had a mixture of names – Priestholm being favoured by the Vikings, while its saintly hermit gave it the name of Ynys Seiriol, and its English name reflects the hoards of birds that were at one time caught, pickled in barrels twelve inches long and sold to England for 3 or 4 shillings a barrel. However, here in 1748, Lewis Morris found a thriving herring fishery. Oysters were also in abundance locally.

In comparison to the rest of Anglesey, the east coast has always had a more vigorous fishery. Around the beginning of the nineteenth century it was said that the herring fishers were active all along the coast from Penmon around to Holyhead, and that the herring 'are in some years, a source of considerable wealth to that part of the island'. About the same time a Mr O. Williams of Llanidan on the Menai Straits introduced the 'Torbay system of trawling' to Caernarfon Bay, and later into Red Wharf and Conwy Bays, which created a sudden influx of trawl-boats from Liverpool and Dublin. This probably led to a development in the local fisheries, encouraging the locals to not merely concentrate on fishing the herring.

Moving anti-clockwise onto the east coast from Penmon, it's a short journey to Red Wharf Bay *(Traeth Coch)*. Here was a busy port in the eighteenth century. Lewis Morris suggested the building of a small pier at an estimated cost of £200, yet his advice was never properly heeded. In 1407 it was reported that the total port dues received were 16s 8d, which represents quite a large sum for such a tiny landing. The name of Traeth Coch – literally *red beach* – comes after the Viking incursion of 1170 when the sands were supposedly running red with blood. Offshore the herrings favoured the sandy bottom, and appeared in large shoals. Lewis Morris recognised this, and he also found a healthy fishery further north at Dulas. However in the latter half of the eighteenth century much of this herring was caught by the men from Moelfre. Moelfre seems always to have produced its own share of seamen who travelled the oceans. In the nineteenth century the village was home to a lifeboat, made famous by the wreck of the Royal Charter in 1859. These same seamen were obviously excellent fishermen, many of them returning home from distant lands to catch herring in the season. Joining these came men from Amlwch and Port Llechog *(Bull Bay)*, and as far away as Cemaes and Cemlyn.

So successful was the Moelfre herring that it was known throughout the Island. The fishermen's wives, and children hawked the fish all over the island, sometimes walking over thirty miles a day. The cry of 'Moelfre herring' is still remembered by old folk today around villages such as Rhosneigr and Aberffraw, and even Holyhead.

The Moelfre men generally used fixed nets in their fishing, unlike the majority of the Cardigan Bay drift-netters, because of the stronger tides. The main season for the herring was between October and February, and many Moelfre men sailed over to the Isle of Man in their open boats to extend their season fishing in Douglas Bay. In the early part of the season they used nets with one inch mesh (12 meshes to the foot) and as the season progressed and the fish got smaller, this decreased to 13 meshes a foot. These nets were some 250 feet long and 10 feet deep.

These nets were taken out on a Monday morning and set. Each boat was owned and crewed by four men, and each man owned two nets. All eight were then shot in one train, using small stones every yard or so along the sole-rope to weight it down. Larger stones each end then served as anchors, while floats were attached on the top rope to keep it in the vertical. Each train was then hauled in the morning, it being lifted bit by bit into the boat, the herring removed and then put over the side again, while the boat drifted down tide. Each set would be completely lifted on a Saturday, as in Moelfre, Sunday fishing was most definitely not practised.

Dick Evans is Moelfre's most renowned lifeboat coxswain

Two views of the beach at Moelfre
photos: author's collection

who saved the crew of the 'Hindlea' from certain death in som of the most hideous seas ever seen, exactly one hundred yea to the day after the 'Royal Charter' was wrecked. For hi bravery in this epic rescue he received the RNLI's gold meda Today, though, he remembers the herring fishing when he wa a kid, when he worked initially with his grandfather off th village beach. In those days, all the town's seamen came hom for the herring, and they spent a month preparing their 16 open boats and setting up nets. The boats were coal-tarre beneath the waterline, and painted white above. Almos immediately afterwards the fishing began, with each boa rowing out to their nets in the early morning. Sometimes th herring shoals were a mile offshore, in about 3 fathoms of wate at low water, while other times they were found off Benllech. T get the few miles there, the small lugsail was used on the boa otherwise mostly he remembers only using the heavy oars.

Benllech had its own fleet of similar herring boats, albe much smaller in number as it proved awkward carrying th boats and herring up the much longer sandy beach. The herrin were often put in sacks, and the boats were brought in with th tide, a time-consuming affair. In later times, a horse and ca was bargained from some local with one to spare.

In later life, when Dick was earning £3 10s as a ship's office he came home to fish the herring. On a good week, whe herring fetched an enormous amount of £3 10s a barrel – equ to his weekly wages remember – upwards of £50 and £60 week could be earned. Even when prices fell to 12s a barrel, good wage was still obtainable. Only when it fell to 5s a barr was this deemed poor.

The wealth created by the herring reflected all around th village. The butcher and the baker benefitted through increase trade, and even the tailor saw an upsurge in business when th young fishermen, not thinking twice about buying a new £5 su to go courting, patronised his meagre shop. Dick recalls th times when he and the other village kids were nickname

*Two views of the beach at Moelfre at the beginning of this century
showing the typical beach boats that were used
in the herring fishery
photos: Anglesey County Record Office*

"Moelfre herrings" when they attended the nearby Llanallg○ school.

Onshore gales were the worst for the herring. This ofte□ threw the stones out of the nets so that they twisted up. Th◦ herring also swam into deeper water. Once the wind abated they would row out to lift the nets, bring them ashore an◦ disentangle them in a nearby field. Women often helped wit□ this task. Mostly, however, the nets only lasted 4 or 5 weeks, a◦ it appeared they were never barked (preserved by soaking i□ oak bark or cutch). Perhaps this was deemed a waste of time a◦ the nets, more often as not, were destroyed. New ones wer◦ then sent for from Musselburgh, near Edinburgh.

The fish was caught in the early morning and landed b◦ about 9 o'clock, so that the hawkers had most of the day to se□ it. After the railway arrived much of the catch was bough□ direct by Liverpool merchants who carried it by horse and car□ and later lorry, to the railhead at Benllech for carriage to th◦ city. This continued up to the 1930's, when large quantities wer◦ so landed and the process of the barter on the beach is still fres□ in the minds of those few able to recall these times. Indeed during the thirties, a special train was chartered to take herrin◦ to the market at Birmingham. Dick still remembers th◦ salesman, one Patrick Hogan, who bought all the herring off th◦ Moelfre fishermen. Once he had completed his dealing on th◦ beach, he paid Dick a further £1 to lift the barrels onto his lorr◦ – each barrel containing over 700 herring. When Dick went o□ strike, Hogan tried to get others to do this, unsuccessfully, an◦ eventually had to re-employ Dick at an increased rate of £2.

Unfortunately the Moelfre fishery did not survive past th◦ outbreak of war in 1939, so that the beach fell silent, the lovel◦ double-ended and transomed clinker boats began to fall apart and in time the tourist and his unfortunate ways replaced th◦ fishermen, his wooden boxes of herring and the general thrill o□ the early morning landing, usually witnessed by most of th◦ village children. It was said that in the heyday of the fishery when the pubs were still deemed a no-go area by the villag◦

elders and women, the local publicans managed more trade in their establishment before 6am than they did afterwards. Indeed, Patrick Hogan is said to have taken all the fishermen into one such pub after the fish were loaded onto his wagon.

Nowadays the one surviving pub by the beach relies mostly on the holidaymaker to replace those days of old. It certainly is difficult to imagine that there were upwards of twenty-five boats working off the beach, all with real-life names like 'Sovereign', 'Seagull', 'Stag' and 'Shramrock'. Yet I'm sure I heard the fishermen's chat as I recently stood and gazed out over the beach, fresh from Dick's front room and with summer's heat at my brow. Their shadows still stand proud over this beach, even though its carpark and plastic boats seem to dominate the whole atmosphere. No doubt their hearts lie buried beneath the pebbles – and if you don't believe me, just listen out yourself one autumn evening as they scrunch their way up from the water's edge, herring in hand, smelling deep of the sea . . . !

Again moving around the Island in an anti-clockwise direction, the next bay from Moelfre is Llugwy where boats found shelter in the lee of the land. Next is Dulas, already mentioned, and then Amlwch, with its tiny cove that, in 1748, was deemed to be unsuitable for visiting craft, and which was later a small fishing port before the discovery of copper which then caused it to develop into a thriving port based wholly on the nearby Parys Mountain mine. Porth Llechog is only a couple of miles west, with its tiny beach that did produce a limited amount of shelter. Nowadays, like Moelfre and many other coastal regions of the island, tourism takes pride of place in the local economy so that the traditional way of life for generations of fishermen and sea-going folk has completely disappeared for good.

The fishermen of Cemaes, a few miles west, were reputedly salting herring prior to the 1820's. Yet there were only a few fishermen, and as we've already seen, most of this herring came

Amlwch harbour in 1997
photo: author

Porth Llechog (Bull Bay) 1997
photo: author

rom the east coast. The seabed all along the north coast is foul
and the tides strong over this rough bottom which makes
ishing particularly hazardous.

A new pier was built in Cemaes in 1835 after the old one was
destroyed by the sea before 1828. The harbour then developed,
mostly in the trade of limestone, stone and coal for the growing
house building, and fishing never really became of any
consequence. In 1922, in a letter, Owen H. Parry of Glanaber,
Penrhyn, Cemaes Bay, mentions of the previous year, 1921, that
the herring fishermen were 'doing quite well here being on a
very small scale'. The port declined in general with the arrival
of the railway at Holyhead and Amlwch, so that today it is
home to a few boats potting for lobsters and crabs, and the
visitor with his slick speed boat and infuriating jetski.

Holyhead is the next harbour as we move around Anglesey.
Here the ferry to Ireland has been running since the mid 1800's,
after it gained preference over Porth Dinllaen as the port of
embarkation. A hundred years earlier Lewis Morris had found
a thriving export of herrings and a multitude of other fish.
Between 1756 and 1758 some 13,802 barrels of red herring were
salted for local consumption at the port. However the fishing
never really developed on a large scale, so that only a few boats
continue to be based there. It did thrive for a very short period
between the wars, but only because of the Scottish drifters that
landed there. Then Scots herring lassies could be found gutting
and packing the fish on Salt Island, prior to the barrels being
sent by train away to the markets. This was repeated, again
briefly, this time by the fishermen from Northern Ireland,
particularly Kilkeel, who landed their herring at Holyhead
during the first part of the 1960's.

In contrast, the west coast of Anglesey never really saw a
fishery of any consequence, although herring were reported as
being plentiful in Caernarfon Bay. Rhosneigr was a tiny,
scattered fishing village of white cottages, typical to Anglesey,
until it was 'discovered' by the English holidaymakers in the
1880's, so that today it is called locally "Little England". Until

The harbour at Cemaes Bay about 1930
showing various transom-sterned boats
photo: author's collection

Boats on the beach at Penrhyn, Cemaes c. 1920
photo: author's collection

then most of Anglesey remained untouched, and increasingly more of these paradise searchers brought themselves onto the island to exploit its beauty during the summer months. And so began their migration that eventually led to the anglicization of much of the traditional Anglesey way of life that today results in huge tracts of the island being home to unsightly caravans and unsympathetic housing. Bringing with them their sense of the English way of life that sometimes is forced upon the unsuspecting Celts, it sure is not surprising that so much resentment exists between the two communities today. This is apparent in many different aspects of daily life, and perhaps the most disgusting of these is the large number of second-homes that remain empty throughout a full 48 weeks of the year while the Island suffers a housing shortage amongst its native population. Mind you, a proportion of blame must be attributed to the local council and its officers who do not always seem to operate in a respectful and honest way!

Rhosneigr, long before this influx, was renowned for its lobsters. In 1600 George Roberts noted that these lobsters were 'very sweete and delicate meate and plentie taken', and, like most of the west and north coasts, these lobsters and crabs were more likely to be landed than herring. Mackerel, later on in the season, was landed in large quantities.

Aberffraw Bay, although Morris had only noted it for its 'oysters, whiting and other fish', supported a herring fishery briefly when this was established by boats from Liverpool and Hoylake, after huge shoals were reported off the west coast in 1884. This disappeared as quickly as it had arrived.

Aber Menai, at the southwest tip of the Island, was said to have been a haven for fishermen in the early nineteenth century, and no doubt some herring was landed at Llanddwyn Is, especially as, at one time, it was a lifeboat station and base to the Caernarfon pilots. At Penlon, near Newborough, on the mouth of the River Braint, the Long Ship Inn was said to have been a haunt of fishermen and smugglers, who drew their vessels up in the river at times. Today illegal salmon fishing possibly plays a more important part than probably herring ever did!

The Fishing Boats

In almost all parts of Anglesey the boats used by the herring fishers were small craft up to some 20ft overall. A print of Beaumaris of about 1835 shows several small transom-sterned craft, each with a square-sail. Similar vessels show in a photograph of Holyhead, although by this time – the end of the nineteenth century – the square-sail had been dropped for the lug sail, as was common with these size of craft all over the West Coast of Britain.

Moelfre, however, was the exception. Here open boats up to 30ft, similar to those from Nefyn, worked from the small beach. These were clinker-built, as were the smaller craft, and displayed a definite Viking ancestry. Mostly these bigger boats were built by Matthews of Menai Bridge, who was a prolific builder of such craft around the turn of this century. The smaller boats were, on the whole, built by local builders around the island, these often being built by people in their homes.

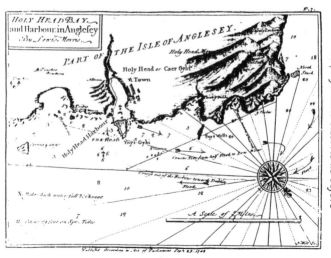

map of Lewis Morris as before

100

CHAPTER 6

The North Wales coast from Caernarfon to the River Dee

Returning by way of Stephenson's Brittania Bridge to the mainland, recently rebuilt after the disastrous fire of 1969, it's only a short hop back to Caernarfon, purposely omitted in previous chapters. Caernarfon has been an important settlement ever since the Romans were here, and probably long before that. It sits at the head of the River Seiont, in a commanding position overlooking the Menai Straits which are about a mile wide at this point. Edward I's castle dominates the harbour, which in 1566 was recognised as being a port with 120 households. Lewis Morris found abundant supplies of salmon, cod, whitings, all kinds of flat fish, oysters, mussels and cockles;

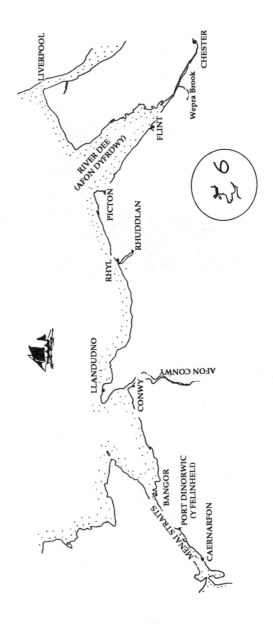

however he made no reference to King Herring. It seems that the harbour, built upon the slate trade from Llanberis, from where the railway came with wagon loads of the material, had a flourishing fishing trade, but one that was, on the whole, based upon trawling. As we saw in the preceeding chapter, trawling was introduced into the area in the early nineteenth century, and these boats soon realised the advantage of landing their catch at the port. However the small herring boats, not wanting to navigate the shifting sands over Caernarfon Bar, which can be treacherous under certain conditions, nor wishing to struggle in tidal conditions up the few miles of the Straits to Caernarfon, continued to land in the rural locations. Afterall, a horse and cart can travel quicker than a boat, especially when wind and tide are against you. Having said that, various mentions have been made of herrings being landed at Caernarfon prior to 1880.

In 1883 there were 300 boats in Caernarfon and its neighbouring creeks. 17 of these were first class boats over 15 tons. By this time, the bigger boats were more concerned with catching herring, and it seems greater quantities of it were landed this century. In 1913 some 1,842 hundredweight were landed there, but this has reduced to 25 cwt within a quarter of a century.

That herring was part of the staple diet of Caernarfonshire rural folk is undisputed. Strings of herring were often to be seen hanging outside the cottages of the poorer people, and this in itself indicates that they were willing to eat the fish whenever it was possible for them to get it. The best fish, however, remained as an exclusive luxury for the very rich.

Port Dinorwig (Y Felinheli) is a harbour again built entirely to export slate. Likewise Penrhyn Dock, at Bangor, was built for the loading of slates from the Bethesda quarry. Both have in common the fact that they were not mentioned by Lewis Morris, although Hirael, a suburb of Bangor had several fishermen working off the shore. Weirs were noted by Hall as catching salmon, herrings and flat-fish. Ten percent of this

Caernarfon Castle and boats c. 1890
photo: Gwynedd Archives

Bangor, from Anglesey
photo: author's collection

catch, he wrote, was the normal rent for such a weir, and examples a recently built weir that cost £800 to build. Herrings, it seems, constituted the chief dependency of the tenant. The herrings taken were sent 'as far away as Shrewsbury and Bridge North, whence regular fish carts arrive in season'. In Hall's time, this herring was selling at some 4 shillings a hundred, while salmon was one shilling a pound. Llandegai, near Bangor, he noted, had a smoke-house built in the early part of the nineteenth century, of which he was said that it 'has proved almost instantaneously a great and extensive advantage to the poor, who are now enabled to buy salted herrings at a reasonable rate'. Vast shoals were reported off Caernarfonshire between Bangor and Conwy in 1883. This improvement of the fishery coincided with a decline in the need for stone setts from the nearby quarries, so fortunately happened when those quarrymen were being laid off.

Conwy is the next place of consequence along the North Wales shore and was noted as a haven in 1566 with threescore households. Fishing continued to play a part in the local trade, although herrings never seem to have figured very much in this. Oak bark was exported from the port up to the nineteenth century, otherwise the estuary seems to have been the most important mussel gathering centre in the whole of Wales.

At Rhosfynach, by the Little Orme head, 'there has existed' wrote D.C. Davies in the 'Sea Fisheries of Wales' for the Liverpool Eisteddfod in 1883, 'for centuries a privileged Weir in which, it is said, large quantities of salmon, cod, whiting, mackerel and herrings are caught'.

Between Great Ormes Head and Rhyl, tourism has been more prevalent. Here the seaside resorts of Llandudno, Rhos-on-Sea (*Llandrillo-yn-Rhos*) and Colwyn Bay (*Bae Colwyn*) blossomed after the railway brought in thousands of sea-searching workers from the Lancashire and Yorkshire industrial towns that flourished in the eighteenth and nineteenth centuries. Although shrimps were on the menu here, herring probably reminded them of being at home, where it was also

The beach at Conwy c. 1890
photo: National Library of Wales

Barrelling herring on the beach at Llandudno
photo: Gwynedd Archives

part of the daily diet. Plenty of sand, sea and amusements led to what is now unkindly referred to as 'Costa Geriatica', the tourism being largely replaced by retired people who find the climate invigorating in their later years of life. Fishermen, no doubt, did exist in these parts, but they probably spent the summer offering the trippers a row around the bay from Llandudno pier.

Y Rhyl, however, although it developed on similar lines in the nineteenth century, was for centuries a tiny fishing hamlet. Its name way back was Foryd, and it was the ancient port of Rhuddlan. The Port Books in 1566 recognise that 'Vorryd adioneth the towne of Rudlan which is a little village so named Rudlan conteyning in it aboute 40 housholdes which are pore people yet non lacking habitacones, which creekes . . . '. In 1800, small fishing boats worked from here and the fishermen lived in 'tiny miserable thatched cottages with turf or cobbled-stone walls' which were in constant threat from the high tides and the sand-dunes. 'Tai-un-nos' – one night cottages – were small cottages that could be erected in one day so that smoke came out of the chimney by sunset. The builder of such a cottage believed that he owned it, and furthermore, if he threw an axe from his door, he believed that he owned all the land encompassed within the radius of this throw. This belief was common throughout rural Wales.

These early fishing boats appear to have been rigged with one square-sail, and they caught all manner of fish. Thomas Pennant, who lived at nearby Mostyn, recorded in 1796 the fishermen as catching 'flounders, plaice, small sole, ray, dab, cod, weaver and even anchovy', as well as mackerel and herring about which he wrote: 'Herrings in this sea are extremely desultory. At times they appear in vast shoals, even as high as Chester. They arrive in the month of November, continue until February, and are followed by multitudes of small vessels which enliven the channel. Great quantities are taken and salted but are generally shotten and meagre. It is now

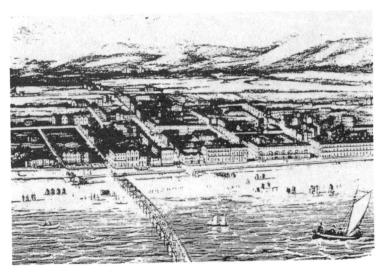

A print of Rhyl

A print of Rhuddlan about 1850

about 10 years since they have paid us a visit.' Large amounts were landed in the years 1766 and 1767.

One record catch is noted in the year 1850 when 35,000 herrings were taken at one go. However, with the development of tourism, fishing declined in the tiny creek, except for a few Morecambe Bay nobbies that landed their shrimps there in summer, boiling the catch in the boilers aboard their boats, and then landing the shellfish and often selling direct to the public.

Along the Dee on the Welsh side, the Port Books give three creeks at 'Picton poole', 'Wepra poole' and 'Welshe Lake'. On today's map these are hardly discernible, although Picton's proximity to the landing at Ffynnongroyw, the bay just inside the Point of Ayre and the Wepra river that runs through Connah's Quay give their ancient positions away. Flint became a fish port, mainly, though, because of the salmon that was landed by the small seine-netters that worked out of both Flint and Connah's quay, and still do. Similar boats net the salmon further upstream at Handbridge in Chester.

Statistics from the Third report of the 1785 Committee on the British Fisheries show that Parkgate, on the English side of the Dee, landed huge amounts of herring between 1766 and about 1780. In the first year of this period there was some 731,220 barrels of both red and white herring salted there for local consumption, which represented a larger amount of fish than was cured at any Welsh port between 1751 and 1782.

In 1883, large shoals were again reported off the Flintshire coast. Hoylake, as we've seen, sent its fleet far afield during the year, but doubtless it worked locally at times. Wallasey, just to the east, at the mouth of the River Mersey, was spoken of as a place 'where men use much to salten herring taken at the sea by the mouth of Mersey', according to John Leland about 1540. Of Liverpool, Andrew Tyrrell, a fish inspector from Liverpool market, told the 1878 Inquiry, 'herrings come here very heavy in Spawn'. He said that he would not allow them to be taken in that state, given the choice, and that very few herrings had been taken that year on the West Coast of England.

The Curing of Herring

Although we have now travelled the complete length of the nearly 600 miles of the Welsh coastline – okay, we missed much of the South Wales coast for lack of any herring – no mention has been made to now of how the herring were actually cured. Generally there were three ways of selling the catch.

Fresh herring

Herring is a fish that deteriorates quickly once it is out of the water. The eyes go dull and grey instead of the bright red eyes that denote fresh fish. Once it is landed in the morning, it has to be taken to market quickly. Obviously, in rural areas where transport was non-existent, this was impossible. As we've seen, local hawkers sold the fish within the immediate rural area around the harbour until, after the arrival of the railway in parts of the Principality, fresh herring could be sent to market on the early morning train.

Also as we've seen, both Aberporth and Nefyn herrings became renowned throughout Wales, and indeed further afield. Hence the cry of the fish salesman around the towns of South Wales was:

Sgadan Aberporth, sgadan Aberporth
Dau fola ac un corff

(Aberporth herrings, Aberporth herrings
Two bellies and one body)

Or similarly the Nefyn cryers:

Penwaig Nefyn, Penwaig Nefyn
Bolia fel tafarnwyr,
Cefna' fel ffarmwrs'

(Nefyn herrings, Nefyn herrings,
Bellies like inn-keepers, backs like farmers.)

Salted herring

Salt's preservative properties have been known for centuries, and herring laid in a barrel between salt has been one of the main ways of enabling the food to be sent to distant markets. More recently, the Scotch cure has proved popular. Bands of Scots girls followed the fishing fleets – the herring lassies as they were called – and they spent their days preparing the herring and laying it into the barrels. Barrels were made by the resident coopers, and the herring tipped directly from the boats into a trough or 'farlane'. The girls then gutted the fish, they being able to gut one every second. The fish were then put into the barrels with salt between each layer. The barrel would then be sealed and left, before it was re-opened and packed tighter after the herring had shrunk. In Scotland, barrels were branded according to the type of fish within the barrel, but this was not common practise in England and Wales.

Smoked herring

Gutted and split herring, if left in a pickle of saltwater for a short period, can then be hung up in a smoke-house and immersed in the smoke of oak chips. This then produces the kipper that we all know. Smoke-houses were generally to be found at any place where herrings were landed and the bigger ports had several. Even in rural areas there would be at least one, and many fishermen kept their own 'backyard' smoker behind their cottage.

However, if the herrings are not split, merely gutted, and then smoked, they became bloaters. Different ways produce different types of bloater. In some parts of Wales, the herring are left in salt for up to three weeks, usually on the floor of the salt-house, after they have been smoked for a short time. They are then washed and salted again, before being dried. In Nefyn they were dried by being laid out on a pile of ferns in the sunshine when, on the rare occasion, the sun shines in the autumn. In other parts of Britain, the ungutted herring are merely smoked whole after being salted.

Red herrings are again not split, but smoked whole after an initial salting. They are normally hung high up in the smoke-house where they receive little smoke. Left there in between daily smokings of kippers, they sweat until the smoker is relit, and they might remain here for up to three weeks, after which they are removed for keeping. The cliche 'red herring' comes from the fact that herrings so preserved were known to put a hound off its scent! They were also renowned for being beneficial in the treatment of gall-stones and rheumatism! Occasionally a fisherman might hang them high up in his chimney at home so that they go through the same process.

The following is a collection of the prices of herring from the Welsh Port Books:

Irish red herrings	– barrel	5s	
	– meise	5s	
Irish white herrings	– barrel	5s	
herrings	– full barrel	10s	
	– last		6d (61?)
herrings shot	– meise	5s	
	– barrel	5s	
	– hogshead	10s	
	– last	31	
Irish cod fish	– 100	30s	
	– copule		6d
ling	– copule	1s	4d
Newfoundland dry	– 100	10s	
salmon	–hogshead	31	
	– dozen	6s	8d

Conclusion

Conclusion

And so we have completed our journey through the pages of hundreds of years of Welsh fishing for the king of the sea. Throughout this journey one thing has become obvious and that is, although the herring fishery of Wales never achieved the notoriety that it did in other places such as Scotland, the Isle of Man or East Anglia, it was a substantial fishery that employed a significant number of the local population within the rural communities. Although these periods of intensity of the fishing were of a relatively short duration – only a couple of months at times – it did provide both an alternative to the regiment of farming and an addition to the otherwise monotonous diet. It brought an influx of merchants into some areas, which in turn led to development of the communities, and gave seamen an excuse to return home for the autumn months. Within the last two hundred years or so the regions of the country also developed their own industries. Flintshire and Denbighshire had their lead mines, collieries and limestone quarries, Anglesey its copper mines, Caernarfonshire and Merionethshire its slate mines, Montgomeryshire and Cardiganshire its lead mines, Carmarthenshire and Glamorgan its collieries, iron and tinplate works, and its copper-smelting, while agriculture figured prominent in East Wales. These all served to provide the rural worker with a source of income, so that the herring was only persecuted as a last resort. As we've also seen, the many seaman who originated from parts of the coast, mostly from Ceredigion and Llŷn, came home to fish as they believed the herring fishery to be an important source of their income, and one that was relatively easily sought.

Yet today the signs remaining of this once great fishery are non-existent. The herring shoals have deserted the coasts, the boats have rotted away and the curing houses have disappeared back to the earth from whence they came. Only memories remain in those few minds that remember, and these are increasingly been taken away by the one final certainty of life. The small creeks remain, with their adaptation into modern day life, and the quays stand still in those few harbours that survived. Yet these represent the tiniest shadow of a way of life that was central to these small communities. I can only say that it has been a pleasure to peer, all too briefly, through distant windows that have allowed me a glimpse of what was simple reality to those of a greater strength that lived these shores before technology interrupted the natural progression of life.

APPENDIX 1

Herring Fishermen's Measurement

1 mease/meise or mwys in Welsh equals 5 Hundred
1 last   equals 100 Hundreds
                                          about 2 tons of herring

The Hundred:

One of the most common measurements, not merely within the fishing, is the Hundred or Long hundred. It probably originated as ten dozens, but has acquired different meanings throughout Britain over the years.

For the herring, one Hundred can be several different measures, depending where you are. In Cornwall it is 132 fish – 33 warps of four fish; while in the Isle of Man it represent 124 fish – 40 warps of 3 fish + 4 tally fish for each 10 warps. Here in Wales there are three possibilities.

One Long hundred about Aberystwyth is counted thus: the fish are counted by the score, so that every second score an additional fish was tossed to one side as a warp. Every sixth score another fish was tossed aside into a different pile as the tally (tale). This, then, meant that for every 6 score – 120 fish – there were 3 warps and 1 tally which makes 124 fish. This method was generally used when counting out by the mease (meise) of 5 Hundred, however when only Hundreds were being counted, the tally was not thrown, hence a Hundred would only be 123 fish. Another source mentions a Long hundred as being 126 fish to add further to the confusion.

Therefore:

1 last equals 123,000 fish or 124,000 in Wales/I-O-M or 132,000 – Cornwall

The Cran measures Act of 1908 stipulated a cran measurement thus:

1 cran equals 37½ imperial gallons
        or 28 stone by weight

a ¼ cran basket was the standard basket to carry 7 stones and would be branded so. After 1908 it was used to land the herring and tally the catch.

APPENDIX 2

List of sail plans of vessels used in the herring fishing:

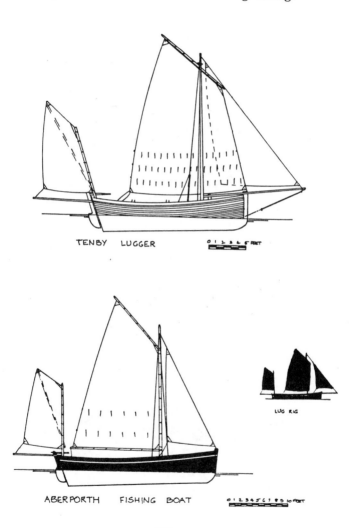

TENBY LUGGER

ABERPORTH FISHING BOAT

LUG RIG

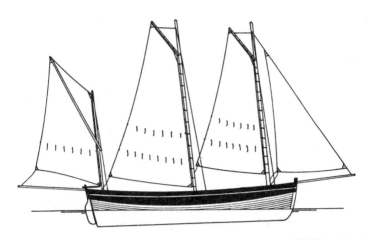

ABERYSTWYTH 3-MASTED BOAT c1880
(CLINKER TYPE)

0 1 2 3 4 5 6 7 8 9 10 FE

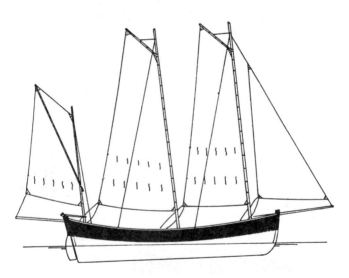

ABERYSTWYTH 3-MASTED BOAT c1880
(CARVEL TYPE)

0 1 2 3 4 5 6 7 8 9 10 FEET

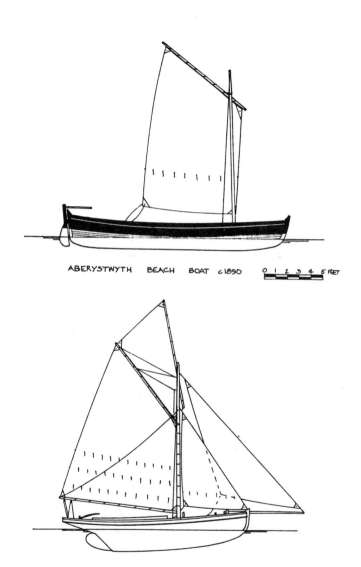

ABERYSTWYTH BEACH BOAT c1890   0 1 2 3 4 5 FEET

MORECAMBE BAY PRAWNER (or LANCASHIRE NOBBY) c1890   0 1 2 3 4 5 6 7 8 9 10 FEET

119

ABERDARON FISHING BOAT c1920

0 1 2 3 4 5 FEET

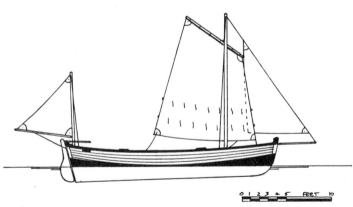

0 1 2 3 4 5 FEET 10

ANGLESEY BEACH BOAT c1890 TYP. MOELRE

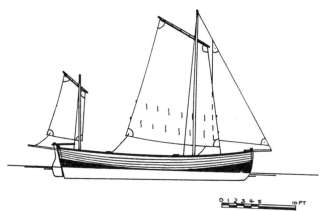

ANGLESEY BEACH BOAT c1920 LUG-RIG-MOELFRE

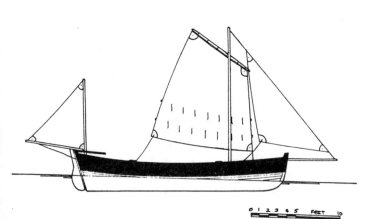

ANGLESEY BEACH BOAT c1890 TYP. CEMAES BAY

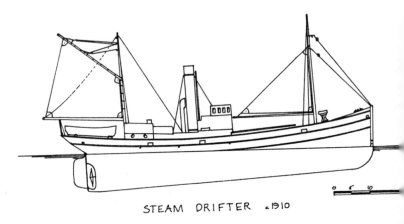

STEAM DRIFTER c.1910

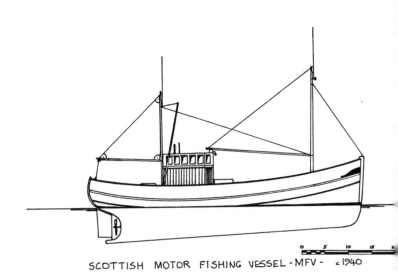

SCOTTISH MOTOR FISHING VESSEL - MFV - c.1940

Statistics of the Welsh herring industry 1750-1782 from Colin Matheson's 'Wales and the Sea Fisheries' (1929):

Year	Holyhead White Ga.	Holyhead White Brls.	Holyhead Red Thousands	Parkgate White Ga.	Parkgate White Brls.	Parkgate Red Thousands	Chester White Ga.	Chester White Brls.	Chester Red Thousands	Beaumaris Red Thousands	Beaumaris White Brls.	Beaumaris White Ga.	Neyland Red Thousands	Neyland White Brls.	Neyland White Ga.	West Wales Red Thousands¹	West Wales White Brls.	West Wales White Ga.	Year
1751	12	4								3,050	11	0	13,950	32	16	60,603	136	13	1751
1752	—	—								14,567	21	16	—	20	25	63,122	123	21	1752
1753										16,513	16	18	41,075	35	18	59,305	188	22	1753
1754		1								7,428	45	4		64	11	50,375	173	21	1754
1755	19		1,550							32,616	36	31	28,920	350	28	42,039	751	13	1755
1756	1		6,662					15		72,184	132	4	11,815	371	28	113,665	471	10	1756
1757	22	33	5,590							78,275	97	15	2,093	120	20	70,675	358	2	1757
1758	10	3								94,750	386	19	50,164	242	0	560,400	276	12	1758
1759	27	9	200							61,959	94	29	4,612	121	18	91,150	252	23	1759
1760	—	8								85,902	240	2	107,287	118	27	62,600	227	26	1760
1761	—	1								57,615	128	29	107,210	42	0	13,150	156	19	1761
1762		—						173		57,825	40	15	105,897	23	19	22,950	93	6	1762
1763								516	79,510	22,987	40	4	44,795	103	30	6,600	149	23	1763
1764		31							7,800	3,775	40	13	15,400	45	21	3,100	99	23	1764
1765										50,050	130	25	100,411	58	20	1,900	127	9	1765
1766				10	3,770	727,450	8			6,928	67	5	185,074	78	4	3,000	333	1	1766
1767				28	308	357,550	16	32		6,289	80	7	662	18	1	5,100	209	16	1767
1768				8	83	119,500				6,937	117	20	1,787	140	30	47,500	882	22	1768
1769				13	6	105,300		1		2,154	57	18		7	1	22,800	1,073	12	1769
1770				9	24	98,900		9		2,445	58	24		28	19	10,900	498	17	1770
1771				6	22	180,175			21,000	187	20	—	60	538	1	2,500	523	26	1771
1772				1	34	125,000		20		1,062	31	16	2,300	779	28	9,000	963	10	1772
1773				2	11	125,680		20		2,325	114	23	450	198	4	6,600	804	30	1773
1774				17	4	138,750		58	12,400	2,300	18	4	350	226	13	11,500	868	6	1774
1775				8	7	105,775	10	54		250	18	27		871	30	14,900	279	28	1775
1776					5	23,500	12		600,000		134	5	155,429	1,083	1	21,450	1,058	28	1776
1777		31			78	26,025				200	122	28		322	7	78,600	1,314	18	1777
1778				—	15	157,600	—	10		375	326	31		61	6	4,500	250	15	1778
1779				2	2	18,250					238	6		79	11	1,700	250	14	1779
1780				—	—	1,500					196	10			16	1,800	279	16	1780
1781	19	43			57	2,300									16	3,800	45	6	1781
1782	16	48																	1782

¹ One "thousand" = 1,320 herrings.
² 32 gallons = 1 barrel.

APPENDIX 4

Number of fishing boats in Wales 1878

Port	Port letter	1st class		2nd class		no. tonnage unknown	3rd class		no. tonnage unknown	total		tot. no. tonnage unknown	men & boys const. employed	others occas. employed
		no	ton	no	ton		no	ton		no	ton			
Aberystwyth	AB	–	–	9	60		68	258		77	318	–	–	267
Beaumaris	BS	7	155	98	220		43	57		148	432		127	222
Caernarfon	CO	17	368	85	381	2	23	24		125	783		184	162
Cardiff	CF	1	15	4	17		9	11		14	43		6	34
Cardigan	CA	–	–	48	212		30	65		78	277		80	322
Chester	CH	–	–	3	5		–	–	6	3	5	8	–	6
Milford	M	14	307	152	435		85	62		251	804		353	112
Swansea	SA	3	42	155	1368		–	–		158	1410		465	21

Interesting points:

1. Aberystwyth had no full-time fishermen.
2. Beaumaris includes Bangor & Holyhead.
3. Second class are mostly herring boats.
4. Chester only had 3 boats – possibly more salmon boats were not included.
5. Cardiff – 3rd class probably cockling boats.
6. The 1902 Regulations for the Registry, Lettering & Numbering of British Fishing Boats under Pt 4 of The Merchant Shipping Act, 1894 & The Sea Fisheris Acts, 1868 & 1883 state:

1st Class, which shall include all steamers of 15 tons gross tonnage and upwards, and all boats (other than steamers) of 15 tons register tonnage and upwards.

2nd Class, which shall include all steamers of less than 15 tons gross tonnage and all boats (other than steamers) of less than 15 tons register tonnage or of 18 ft keel and upwards.

3rd Class, which shall include all boats under 18ft keel, other than those navigated by oars only and marked in accordance with Section 176 of the Customs Consolidation Act, 1876. (This states that all boats under 100 tons, except registered fishing boats, must have the name of the owner and the port painted outside the stern.)

40 + FISHING BOAT ASSOCIATION

OF THE BRITISH ISLES

– founded by Mike Smylie and Michael Craine in 1995 – it is open to anyone with an interest in fishing boats

Aims: 1) To encourage awareness of our Maritime Heritage with special regard to the fishing industry of the past.
2) To represent owners of such vessels.
3) To encourage research in the historical and social elements of fishing boats, and to encourage liaison between boat owners, museums, heritage centres, trusts, businesses, similar organisations, fishermen and individuals.
4) To encourage restoration of such vessels before it is too late.
5) To act as a link between similar organisations in the European Union.
6) To lobby Government to recognise the importance of our Maritime Heritage, and to act upon it before it is too late.

The association endeavours to be non-profit making, and the current cost is £7 per year which covers the cost of 3 newsletters a year entitled 'Fishing Boats'.

Contact:
MICHAEL CRAINE, "HILLCREST", 63 BIRCHILL CRESCENT, ONCHAN, ISLE OF MAN, IM3 3DA
Tel: 01624 627568 or 01248 430708

Welsh Heritage Series

An informative series of books full of interesting facts and illustrations, presenting Wales, its history, its folklore, its character and its language.

1 Shrouded Quays (Lost Ports of Wales)
– Aled Eames. 96 pp; ISBN 0-86381-197-3; many illustrations; **£2.50**

2 Welsh Pub Names
– Myrddin ap Dafydd. 84 pp ISBN 0-86481-185-X; many illustrations; **£2.50**

3 Traditional Fishing in Wales
– Emrys Evans. 72 pp; ISBN 0-86381-320-8; many illustrations; **£3.50**

4 A History of the Red Dragon
– Carl Lofmark. The national symbol of Wales through the ages.
ISBN 0-86381-317-8; **£3.50**

5 A Guide to Welsh Place-Names
– Anthony Lias. ISBN 0-86381-289-9; **£3.50**

NEW FOR 1998:

6 The Herring Fishers of Wales
– Mike Smylie. A journey, following the 'silver darlings' along the coast of Wales, calling at the different ports and small harbours, retelling the history of the herring fisheries in Wales. 128 pp; ISBN 0-86381-467-0; **£3.75**

7 A Study of Radnorshire Place-names
– Richard Morgan. 96 pp; ISBN 0-86381-487-5; **£4.50**

8 Welsh Nots, Welsh Notes and Welsh Nuts
A dictionary of phrases using the word 'Welsh' by T.B. Edwards.
ISBN 0-86381-485-9; **£4.75**